Bright Ideas
Maths Games

Written by Rosemarie Brewer and Marion Cranmer

Published by Scholastic Publications Ltd,
Marlborough House, Holly Walk,
Leamington Spa, Warwickshire CV32 4LS.

© 1988 Scholastic Publications Ltd.
Reprinted in 1989 ,1990 ,1990

Written by Rosemarie Brewer and
Marion Cranmer
Edited by Jane Hammond
Sub-edited by Melissa Bellamy
Illustrations by Jane Bottomley

Printed in Great Britain by
Loxley Brothers Ltd, Sheffield

ISBN 0 590 70874 0

Front and back cover: designed by Sue Limb,
photographs by Martyn Chillmaid

Contents

Rockets and Comets

Introduction

As practising infant class teachers, we feel that games could be valuable within the school curriculum, and we have become increasingly enthusiastic about the part they might play in the teaching of mathematics.

The whole staff of our school were particularly interested in improving the standard of mathematics, and so a maths consultant was brought into school for one day a week for an initial period of one year, to work alongside teachers in their classes and with groups of teachers in staff meetings. The extra stimulus and encouragement provided by the consultant helped so much that the length of stay was increased to three years. By working closely together, examining the content and purpose of our maths games, we were able to improve them. We have continued to make games with our classes and integrate them into our teaching strategies since that time.

FULFILLING PUPILS' NEEDS

The Cockcroft Report, *Mathematics Counts*, states that, 'All pupils need opportunities to practise skills and routines which have been acquired recently, and to consolidate those which they already possess, so that these may be available for use in problem-solving and investigational work.' Obviously the amount of practice that individual children need varies greatly. By playing and replaying a selection of games, children who take longer to grasp ideas can practise and reinforce skills, gain concepts and develop problem-solving strategies in a way that they can enjoy. The enthusiasm and pleasure shown by the children when playing maths games enhances their attitude towards the subject, and the active involvement necessary to play aids their learning.

Cockcroft also argues that, 'The primary mathematics curriculum should enrich children's aesthetic and linguistic experience, provide them with the means of exploring their environment and develop their powers of logical thought, in addition to equipping them with the numerical skills which will be a powerful tool for later work and study.' Discussions provoked by the games help children to organise their thinking and to build links from meaningful practical activities towards abstract mathematical ideas. Oral assessment in secondary school maths exams has increased the need for children to be able to verbalise their ideas with confidence.

Mathematics 5–11 stresses the importance of co-operation in mathematical learning. In a game situation co-operation is

the pork butcher

necessary, even if the game is of a competitive nature. Games help children who tend to work alone to be involved with at least one other person, and relationships within the class are improved.

CREATING THE GAMES

Games may originate in a number of ways: from a certain part of the maths curriculum that you wish the children to learn; from the topic being studied in the class; from a particular situation, book or object. For example, the 'Broomsticks' game originated in a class where measurement of length needed practice, 'Rockets and comets' developed from a class topic about space, 'Spotty faces' was made during a chicken pox epidemic, 'Sleepy sheep' was inspired by the book, and 'Coily snakes' came about because there had to be a use for the toy snakes that the children kept bringing into school. However the games originate, they must be relevant to the children, and developed with the children where possible.

It is valuable to make a prototype of the game to play and discuss with the children. This enables you to modify the content and rules and to incorporate more of the children's ideas before making the final version. It is important to use the children's illustrations when you make a game, since this motivates them to play and to take great care of the game and its pieces. Home-made games using illustrations by and of the children can avoid racist or sexist messages, and any problems which arise can be discussed.

Attractive presentation makes games more eye-catching and gives them high prestige in the class. The children can achieve a high standard of presentation if they use good quality paper and card in a range of colours and sizes, and felt-tipped pens of different thicknesses in a variety of colours. The games must be covered with a protective self-adhesive film or laminated to make them more durable. Even when using high-quality materials, the cost of producing home-made games is far less than buying commercially produced games.

PLAYING THE GAMES
Through experience we have found that most games are played more successfully by two children only, unless there is supervision. This helps to avoid the common argument about whose turn it is. All the games in this book are suitable for two players unless specifically stated otherwise. An adult or an older child could supervise and may help children to learn how to play a new game. Whoever teaches the game must play it from start to finish with the class teacher to ensure that they have a common understanding of the rules and ideas involved.

Children may want to borrow games to take home in the same way that they borrow books, with similar record-keeping and school-home discussion. As written recording is not appropriate to all games it is especially important that the teacher keeps a record of the games played in school and the types of responses made by the child.

Some children are frustrated by games of pure chance, but an *element* of chance allows less able children to achieve success. Games can be structured so that they involve chance or skill or a combination of both. A single game can be played in several ways by using different sets of cards, or dice, or even pieces as in 'Santa's store'. A simple track game may have the number of moves indicated by:
- magic beans (see 'Hints and tips'),
- a large die with spots,
- a numeral die,
- two dice added together,
- the difference between two dice,
- cards with clues appropriate to the ability of the children (for example, '2 plus 1', '6 multiplied by 0.5', '12 divided by 4', 'the third prime number').

By varying games in this way, a favourite game can be played profitably over a number of months or even years. It is important that children realize that the rules of a game may be changed as long as they are agreed by all players.

STORAGE AND ACCESSIBILITY
Sensible storage and accessibility are essential if the games are to be used over a period of time. If there is enough space in your classroom the children can be encouraged to play games by leaving some out on display, which should be changed regularly. Even in the smallest classroom there is usually space to hang a few baseboards on a small hook on the wall. Suitable storage for games may range from empty chocolate boxes to boxes designed and purchased for that purpose (see 'Hints and tips' for more details).

The games in this book are just a few examples of those which we have created and used in our school. We would encourage you to alter and develop the games to make them more appropriate for your children and to use these ideas as starting points for creating games with the children you teach.

Rosemarie Brewer and Marion Cranmer

Sets

Sorting and classifying helps children to organise their environment. In order to do this they have to think analytically and express their thoughts clearly. They have to recognise that a set is a collection of things which go together and have an attribute in common (for example, the colour red). The attributes that are focused on in the games in this chapter include colour, weather, shape or 'belonging to the set of a frog's dinner'!

Children tend to be involved in sorting on a day-to-day basis, often without realizing it. They are sorting and classifying every time they put away their clothes or toys, every time they recognise a dog or a cat. At school they are sorting when they get into class groups or into groups with different attributes, such as wearing red jumpers.

A teacher can easily introduce correct mathematical language into this type of situation: for example, 'children with red jumpers' can be described as 'the set of children with red jumpers'. Many teachers are unsure about sorting. Some feel confident sorting for colour, shape or size, but do not know how to progress from there. Others begin to use symbols and complicated diagrams far too soon, neglecting to lay thorough foundations.

Many restrict themselves to manufactured sorting materials but these tend to be rather limited. A box of assorted items may have far more potential. For example, a toy rubber gorilla may be sorted into any of the following sets (you could probably think of many more):
- rubber things,
- things that bend,
- things with four legs,
- hairy things,
- things that are taller than a stated object,
- things that are not shiny,
- things that do not have wheels.

This type of sorting and resorting leads naturally into the categories of 'is' and 'is not' or 'has' and 'has not'. The 'Traffic wardens' game is an example of this type of sorting. It also introduces the idea of an item belonging to more than one set at a time (intersection).

Do not forget to introduce the idea of sets with no members. This type of set may occur in 'The posting game' and 'Traffic wardens'.

All the games are for two players unless specifically stated otherwise.

The posting game

For two or more players

What you need
4 baseboards of different colours, 15 letters, a die with four faces coloured to match the 'houses' (baseboards) and two white faces, copies of page 84.

How to play
This game is played co-operatively and not competitively. The baseboards are shared and so do not 'belong' to any one player.

The players take turns to throw the die. The player who throws the die 'posts' a letter to the house of the colour indicated by the die. If a white face is thrown the player misses a turn.

When all the letters have been posted, the houses can be ordered according to the number of letters they have received.

The result of the game can be recorded on the photocopied sheet, one for each child. The children colour the houses on the sheet to match the baseboard cards, and then record the number of letters posted to each house by drawing either coloured dots or letters above each one.

The sheet can then be cut into vertical strips and the strips put in order according to the numbers received by each house – the least to the most or the most to the least. The sheets could be produced with numbers up the side to show how many letters each house has received.

Notes
This game is very popular if Christmas, birthday or other celebration cards are used. The number of letters can be adjusted according to the number of players and/ or their attention span.

For very young players just one sheet could be used with the cardboard letters placed directly on to the sheet from the baseboards.

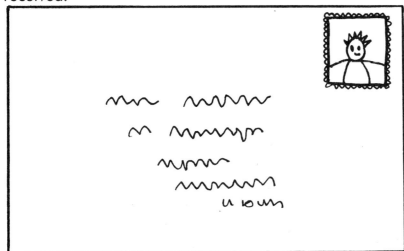

Front and back view of a letter for children to make.

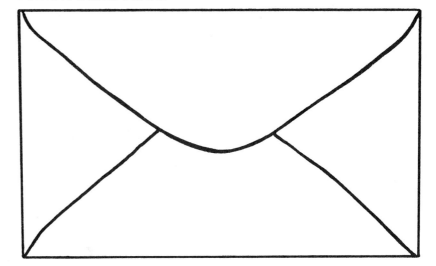

Ask the children to draw the houses in colour, and then mount them on card of the same colour.

Weather sets

What you need
A set of cards (playing card size) comprising: 4 cloud cards, 4 raindrop cards, 4 sun cards, 4 wind cards, 4 snowman cards, 4 frost cards (use glitter or a glitter pen to make the frost on the trees), a hexagon-shaped spinner (six weather pictures on one side and the words on the other) – see page 85 for template.

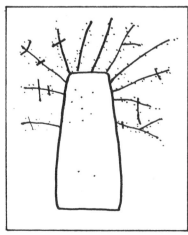

How to play
Game 1
The aim is to collect a set of six different weather cards.

Shuffle the cards thoroughly and deal out six cards to each player. The first player picks up one card from the top of the pack and either discards it or keeps it. If he keeps it, he discards one card from his hand. The discarded card is placed face up next to the pack on the table.

Players take turns to pick up and throw away cards from either pile until they have a complete set of six different cards. The first player with a set wins the game.

Game 2
The aim is to collect a set of four weather cards that are the same. In this game deal four cards to each player and play as Game 1.

Game 3
Sort the cards into six sets. Players start without any cards and then use the spinner to decide which card they may have. As play continues, the spinner may point to a card which the player already has, in which case she misses a turn.

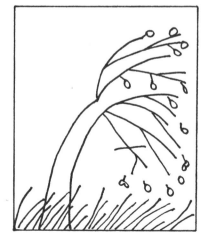
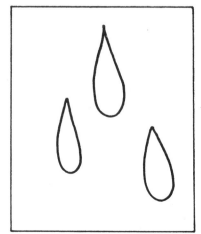

The first player with a complete set of six cards is the winner.

Game 4
Shuffle the cards thoroughly and spread them out face down on the table. In turn, each player turns over one card, which he either keeps or turns face down. The game continues in this manner until one player wins by completing a set of six cards.

Get the children to draw the illustrations for the cards and spinner.

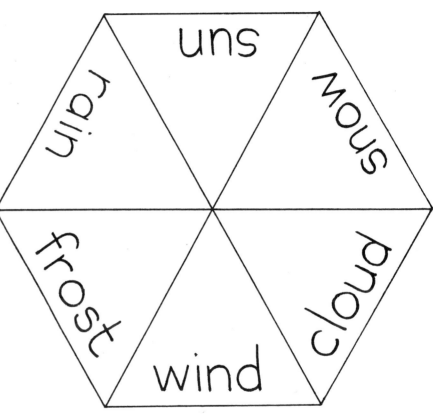

Game 5
Shuffle the cards thoroughly, spread them out face down on the table and play as in the previous game, but this time decide which set of four cards is to be collected (for example, four frosty trees or four snowmen). The winner is the first player to collect a set of four cards.

Rainbow ladybirds

What you need
A baseboard, 2 ladybirds (one with spots and the other with stripes, both to match the colours of the ladybirds on the baseboard), 2 worksheets (copy page 86), 5 magic beans or a 0–5 die (see 'Hints and tips' on page 79), felt-tipped pens.

How to play
Each player has a worksheet and a ladybird which she places on an empty leaf on the baseboard. Players take turns to throw the beans or die and move their ladybird according to the number thrown either way around the board.

If a player lands on one of the ladybirds she ticks the corresponding ladybird on her worksheet.

Continue in this manner until one of the players has ticked all the ladybirds on her sheet, winning the game. Players may then colour the ladybirds on their worksheets the correct colour.

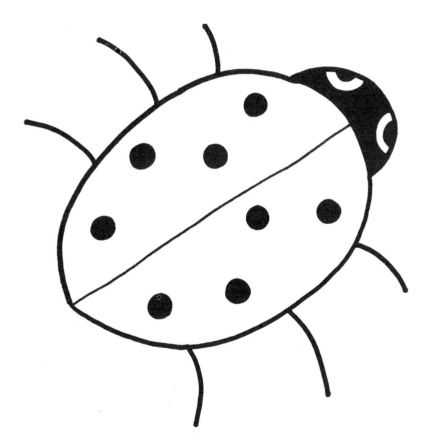

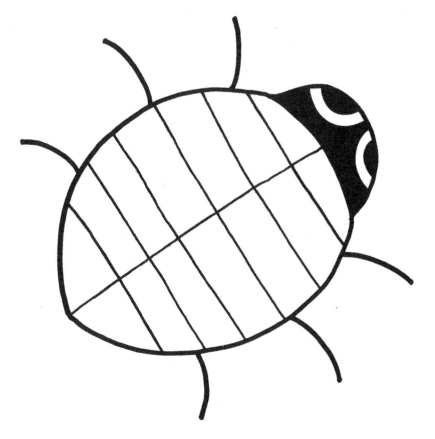

Children can draw and decorate the baseboard, and make the two ladybirds.

Mix a spell

What you need
A baseboard (see page 87), 9 plastic bugs, 2 witch markers, a 1–6 die.

How to play
To start the game, place all the bugs inside the cavern and a witch marker on each cauldron. The players throw the die in turn in order to fly along the star path and collect a bug to bring back to their cauldron. When a bug has been collected the player can put it straight into his cauldron – it does not have to be brought back along the star path.

The winner is the first player to collect five bugs. At the end of the game, get the children to match the bugs they have collected, one to one, in order to find out who has more, who has fewer, and what the difference is.

Notes
Plastic bugs can be purchased from most toy shops. The witches can be made using small polystyrene balls and thin cardboard cones (see figure 1).

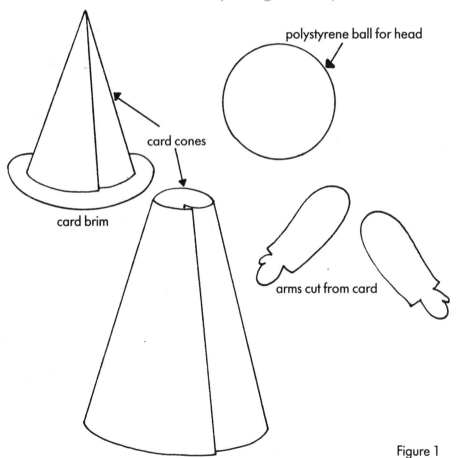

polystyrene ball for head

card cones

card brim

arms cut from card

Figure 1

stick on features, or mark with spirit pen

wool hair

Hungry frog

What you need
A baseboard,
2 counters,
2 hungry frog worksheets
(copy page 88)
illustrated with the same
minibeasts as the
baseboard,
felt-tipped pens or crayons,
a 1–6 die.

The bugs drawn on the baseboard
must match those on the hungry frog
worksheet.

How to play
The players place their counters on any empty leaf ie any
leaf without a minibeast picture on it, and then take turns
to throw the die and move their counters in either
direction along the branch.

If the counter lands on a leaf occupied by a minibeast,
the player ticks off that minibeast on his hungry frog
sheet. The winner is the first player to tick all the
minibeasts on their sheet.

At the end of the game the players could colour in their
sheets.

Notes
This is obviously a pre-number-line game as well as a
sets game. To avoid difficulty in counting on or back
along the branch, make sure that the leaves are well-
spaced.

This game can be altered to fit in with many topics. For
instance, at Hallowe'en the basic game idea can be used
to play 'Collect a spell'. The same rules apply, but in this
case witch or wizard counters are moved forward or
back along a line of planets to collect the ingredients for
a Hallowe'en spell.

Traffic wardens

What you need
A baseboard (see pages 89 and 90), a set of small logiblocks, parking tickets, a traffic warden's hat, a chinagraph pencil.

How to play
Before the game, write sorting instructions at each road junction on the board in chinagraph (for example, 'triangles' and 'not triangles'). Traffic lights remind the players to stop and think.

One player takes each logiblock in turn and 'drives' it to the end of the appropriate road according to the signs. The other player (wearing the traffic warden's hat) then checks that all pieces are 'parked' correctly. Parking tickets may be issued for any pieces that are incorrectly parked. The players then change roles, the sorting instructions are changed and the game proceeds as

before. The winner is the player with the least number of parking tickets.

The game may be made more demanding by adding to the sorting instructions on a new baseboard with a more complex road system (see page 90).

PARKING TICKET

· OFFICIAL ·

for parking in the wrong place

Parking tickets can be made by the children with appropriate instructions and 'fines'.

Notes
The logiblocks are available under various names from educational suppliers.

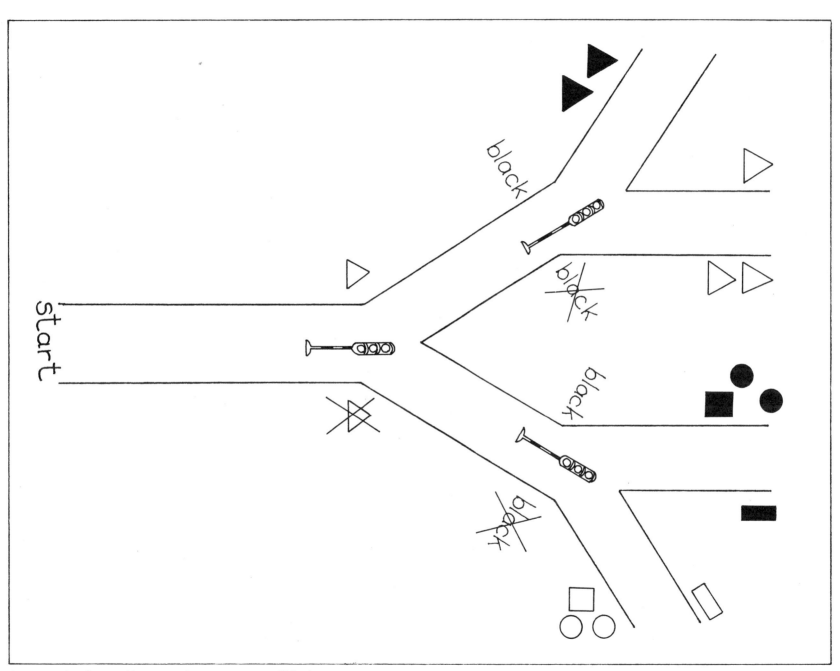

An example of a road layout with instructions and blocks in position.

Number

Children need to understand and be able to manipulate numbers in order to use them as a mathematical tool. Being able to count accurately is necessary to this understanding and manipulation.

Ideas about number will have been formed through working with sets of objects and learning number names. This understanding can be extended by helping children to use number lines. The combination of the sets model and the number line model helps children towards a greater understanding of the consistency of our number system. Using a number line accurately is a skill that needs to be taught – where to begin and end, and how to move forward and back along the line. Pre-number-line games, such as 'Butterflies in the garden', enable children to enjoy learning these skills without being distracted by written numbers.

Through playing games children become familiar with the language of number, and words such as 'more', 'fewer' and 'difference' become much more relevant when applied to a game such as 'Dogs and bones'.

By repeatedly playing with numbers of objects in different configurations and settings children learn about the concept of conservation of number. In games such as 'Spotty faces' and 'Spotty dragons' they begin to

learn that subtraction is the inverse of addition, while in games like 'Hopscotch' they are able to use a variety of operations in order to achieve one result – juggling numbers for fun.

All of these games involve practice in recognition of numerals, which children may use when recording the results of their game. We have suggested some ways of recording but children may find their own ways.

The concept of place value must be introduced to children in order for them to develop an understanding of the decimal number system. They should be made aware that any number may be represented by using a combination of symbols selected from a set of only ten symbols (0 to 9). A number that contains these symbols will be given a name that relates only to that number. For example, the number 55 is 'fifty-five', not 'five five'.

For young children, the concept of place value is easier to explore if a base smaller than ten is used. Counting smaller numbers is easier and quicker and the groupings are more easily recognised by the eye, with incorrect groupings easier to see.

Early experience of place value games should involve the keeping and collecting of groups so that the children can see how small groups can be regrouped. For instance, in the 'Ladybird game', groups of spots are kept throughout so that the number of spots needed to make a family of spotty ladybirds can be seen at the end of the game.

The children should then have practical experience of collecting and exchanging. For instance, if using manufactured base ten materials, they should realize that they can exchange ten units for a ten stick.

Finally, when recording such operations, the children should come to understand the importance of zero as a position holder.

All the games in this chapter are for two players.

Spotty faces

made 1 copy

What you need
A baseboard showing two faces, 40 counters, a 1–6 die.

How to play
This game originated when some members of the class had chicken pox.

Each player plays on one face on the baseboard. The counters are shared equally and put on the faces. Players take turns to throw the die, removing the counters according to the number thrown.

The winner is the first player to remove all the counters from his face, and so recovering from the illness.

Older children can record the game as it progresses using subtraction sums.

The faces must be drawn very large to make room for the counters.

Spotty dragons

What you need
A baseboard, 40 counters, a 1–6 die.

As for 'Spotty faces', make sure the dragons on the baseboard are large enough to take the counters.

How to play
Each player plays on one dragon on the baseboard. They take turns to throw the die, putting counters on their dragon according to the number thrown.

The game is over when all the counters have been used up, and the winner is the player whose dragon has the most spots.

Older children can record the game as it progresses using addition sums.

This game originated after reading *Three Squeaky Dragons* by U Daniels and J Coop from Granada Television's *Let's Go Maths* series.

Hopscotch

What you need
A baseboard (see page 91), two 1–6 dice, 2 hopping children markers.

How to play
Players take turns to throw both dice. They must move on to the numbers in sequence to proceed up the hopscotch spaces, using one or both of the numbers thrown, adding the two numbers together to use the total or using the difference between them. Two consecutive numbers can be used in order. For example, if a 2 and a 3 are thrown

Figure 1

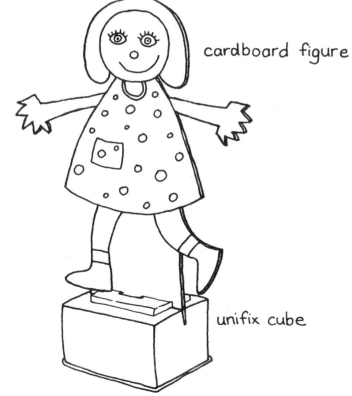

cardboard figure

unifix cube

Figure 2

old penny

and the player is on the 1 space, she may hop on to the 2 and straight away on to the 3 space.

The first player to hop to the end is the winner.

Notes
To make the cardboard figures stand upright you can slot them into Unifix cubes which have cuts in the top. A little Plasticine pressed inside the cubes will stop the figures falling over (see figure 1). (Make sure the Unifix is the soft rather than the brittle variety.) The figures can also be stuck to the fronts of wooden beads or on old pennies (see figure 2).

Butterflies in the garden

made copy

What you need
A baseboard with an odd number of flowers,
2 cardboard butterflies (different colours),
a 1–6 die.

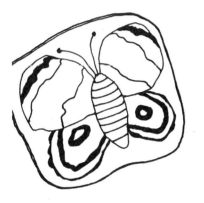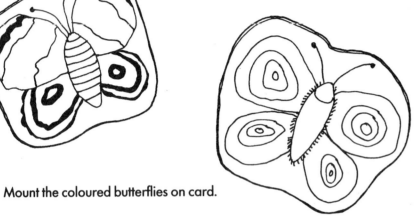

Mount the coloured butterflies on card.

How to play
The players place their butterfly markers on the flower at the extreme left of the baseboard, then use the number die in turn to progress towards the extreme right of the board. The winner is the first player to reach the extreme right-hand flower.

This pre-number game may be extended by asking the players to:

● move from the left to the right and then back to their starting points,

● find the middle flower and move towards opposite ends of the board,

● move from opposite ends towards the middle flower.

The baseboard drawn to scale — each child can draw a flower.

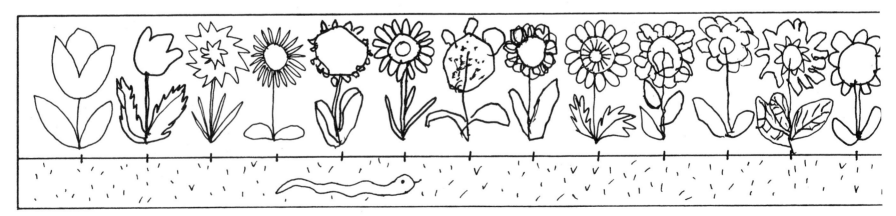

...bers 1 to 4
...r, 2 small
..., a 1–6
...0 Lego bricks
...f the

Two lorries (different colours).

How to play

Shuffle the cards and place them face down on the baseboard. Players place their lorries anywhere on the track to start, then take turns to throw the die to move around the board in a clockwise direction.

When a player has moved her lorry, she picks up a card, and takes the number of Lego bricks indicated by the card combined with the number landed on: for example, 4 lots of 2.

The card is replaced face down at the bottom of the pack, and play continues until all the bricks are used up. The winner is the player with more bricks.

To develop the game further, when the die is thrown players may choose the direction in which to move their lorry, requiring them to work out two possible combinations.

Get the children to illustrate the basic baseboard.

Fly to mother

What you need
A cardboard wall with trees, 2 mother birds, 10 baby birds, number indicators 2–12, two 1–6 dice.

How to play
Game 1
Each player places a mother bird on his end of the wall, takes a number indicator and places it on the grass below his mother bird. The baby birds are shared equally between the players and placed on the grass, then the players take turns to throw the two dice. If the total shown on the dice is the same as their indicator, the player may fly a baby bird up to its mother.

The winner is the first player to collect five baby birds.

Game 2
Play as Game 1, but if the total shown on the dice matches either indicator, the player who threw the dice 'flies' a baby bird to the mother bird above that indicator. This is a less competitive game.

Notes
To make the birds, use large and small dolly pegs. Drill small holes to stick the tail feathers into, and cut slight grooves into the front of the pegs to help the cardboard beaks stick more firmly (see figure 1). If two sizes of pegs are not available, use polystyrene balls to make larger heads for the mother birds. The wall can be drawn on the inside edge of a cardboard storage box and the trees clipped on (see figure 2).

Figure 1

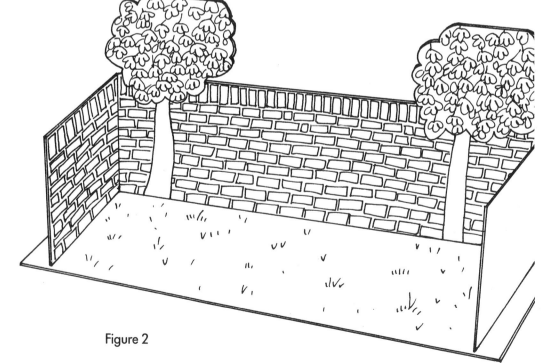

Figure 2

Bunches of flowers

What you need
A box of flowers,
2 worksheets (copy page 94),
wire ties (the kind used
to close plastic lunch bags),
thin felt-tipped pens,
a 1–6 die.

How to play
Players take turns to throw the die taking flowers
according to the number thrown and placing these on the
'flowers' section of the worksheet. When a player has ten
flowers these are tied together to make a bunch, then
transferred to the 'bunches' section on the worksheet
(keeping any spare flowers).

When all the flowers have been won, the players
count the bunches and the flowers and write their totals in
the space provided. The winner is the player with more
flowers. The players should then draw the bunches and
flowers on the worksheets in the places provided.

The game could be extended by collecting ten bunches
of flowers to fill a basket.

Notes
This is a place value game for base ten. It could be used
for other bases by adjusting the number of flowers
required to make a bunch: for example, eight flowers to a
bunch for base eight.

On the sheet the positioning of the boxes in which to
write the number of bunches and the number of flowers
should lead the children towards an understanding of
place value.

Card flowers stapled to milk straws are very quick to make.

Dogs and bones

What you need
A baseboard (see page 95), 2 toy dogs, a 1–6 die, cardboard bones.

How to play
Each player has a dog which is placed on a kennel, and the bones are placed on the dustbin. The players take turns to throw the die and progress towards the dustbin where they collect a bone to take directly back to their kennel. When all the bones have been collected the players match them one-to-one to find out who has more. That person is the winner.

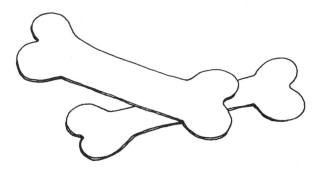

As with many track games, this game can be played at different levels. For younger children magic beans can be used, while older children could use numeral dice or two dice added or subtracted (see Introduction).

Children could add their own illustrations to the baseboard, and make the cardboard bones.

Ladybird family

What you need
2 baseboards (see page 96), 10 Plasticine ladybirds, black pegs for the spots, 2 worksheets (copy page 86), thin felt-tipped pens, a 1–4 die, a chinagraph pencil.

How to play
Each player takes a baseboard. Players take turns to collect spots (pegs) by throwing the die. When a player has collected five or more spots he may take a ladybird, attach five spots to it, and place it in the correct column of the board, keeping any spare spots in the spots column.

Continue in this manner until five ladybirds have been collected, which can then be placed on the leaf. The winner is the first player to win a family of five ladybirds.

The results of the game can then be pictorially recorded on the worksheets.

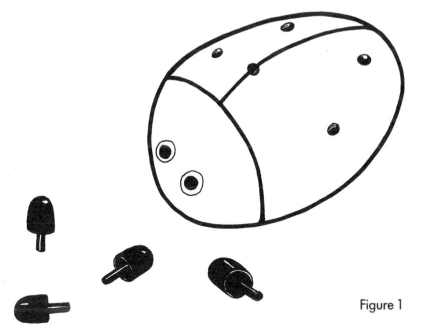

Figure 1

Notes
If the ladybirds are made by the children they are more likely to be looked after and can last quite some time (see figure 1). The holes ready for the spots (pegs) should be made prior to use.

Measures

When babies begin to explore the world around them they also begin to acquire the related language. Children therefore come to school with many ideas about measures, and by giving them more experiences with the correct mathematical language we can help to extend their understanding, and to develop the associated skills.

Cockcroft states that, 'Some children will acquire facility in measurement and in the use of drawing instruments without difficulty, but others will require a long time and much practice to achieve reasonable competence. This time needs to be provided over a period of years.'

Children need to learn to use measuring instruments with reasonable accuracy, although the instruments themselves impose limitations on accuracy when measuring continuous quantities. Encourage them to estimate before measuring accurately.

When they measure length (or height or width) they start by simply comparing two objects: for instance, 'the worm is longer than the caterpillar'. They then progress to more than two objects, such as 'the worm is longer than the caterpillar but shorter than the snake.'

Children should start with non-standard units of measurement which are unequal, such as chalks or pencils. By finding out that the table could be six, ten or fifteen pencils wide depending on the pencils used, the children should begin to see the need for equal units of measurement; in the early stages these could be such things as Unifix bricks or straws. By stating that a piece of string is more than six bricks long, but less than seven bricks long the children will also begin to realise that we need to subdivide units.

When children are introduced to standard measurements of length, help them to see the link between metres, decimetres and centimetres, and hundreds, tens and units, and that a rule can be used as a number line.

Children need a great deal of practice in positioning the ends of items to be compared (a), and in measuring exactly from the edge of an object (b).

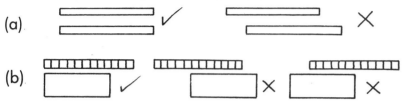

They also need hands-on experience of flexible objects to help them to understand conservation of length: for instance, the length of a piece of ribbon is not altered by rolling it up or tying it in a box. 'Coily snakes' and 'Longest line' provide this type of practice.

Children not only need experience of measuring things around them but also of constructing things of given measurements, such as cutting a piece of string exactly 10½ cm long. They also need to understand that weight is not necessarily indicated by size. For example, small objects may be heavier than large objects, and objects of

the same size may have different weights. This may be experienced in 'Santa's store'.

When measuring capacity children have to understand that a container must be empty to start with and then filled without spillage until it is exactly full. The 'Raindrops' game gives practice in this.

Children need to try covering surfaces and fitting shapes together before they begin to measure area. They need to appreciate that area refers to the whole of a surface, 'across the middle and right up to the edges without any gaps'. 'Hide and seek' demonstrates this.

Time is difficult to learn about, since it cannot be seen or touched. Anything with a steady motion can be used to measure elapsed time, such as a drum beat, a sand timer, a kitchen timer or a clock. Many young children do not realise that analogue clocks can be used for measuring as well as telling the time. Although digital clocks can be read more accurately, they do not give the feeling of time passing as do the hands moving round an analogue clock face.

By using timers for 'Beat the clock' and 'Shape match', the children are helped to 'feel' the passage of a set amount of time. 'Beat the clock' also helps children to understand the structure of an analogue clock face.

Money can be thought of as a numerical system and as a measurement of value or cost. Children need to be able to recognise and sort coins and to understand how many of one type of coin equals the value of another. The skill of counting on is useful when giving change, and the decimal point is often introduced in relation to money.

The 'Lots of money' game gives practice in the recognition and sorting of coins, the addition of money and the convention of recording using a decimal point in the total.

Apart from 'Beat the clock', all the games in this chapter are for two players only.

Longest line

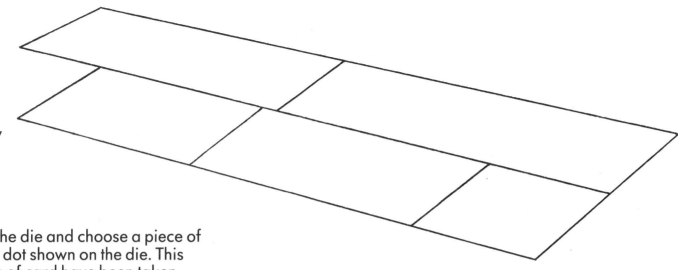

What you need
Strips of card of equal
width in six colours
cut into various lengths
(see page 97 for templates),
a die with six coloured dots
to match the card
colours.

How to play
Players take turns to throw the die and choose a piece of
card the same colour as the dot shown on the die. This
continues until all the pieces of card have been taken,
each player placing his pieces of card end to end. If there
are no pieces of card left of the correct colour, the player
misses that turn. The winner is the player who constructs
the longest line.

Notes
For comparison make sure all the strips are placed edge
to edge and that the beginning of each line starts at the
same place.

Coily snakes

What you need
A baseboard covered with laminate or tacky back,
7 or 8 plastic jointed snakes of different lengths in a box,
2 different-coloured chinagraph pencils, a tissue.

How to play
Make sure the snakes are coiled up in the box, and tell the children that when they remove a snake from the box they must not uncoil it. One player takes a snake, the length of which is estimated by all the players; do this by drawing a line with the chinagraph pencil on the snake outline shown on the baseboard. Then they uncoil the snake and lay it on the baseboard; the player whose estimate is the closest keeps the snake.

Rub out the chinagraph lines with the tissue before repeating this process with the next coiled snake. Continue in this way until all the snakes have been used. The winner is the player with the most snakes.

Notes
These snakes can be bought at most toy shops and are easily dismantled and reassembled into various lengths.

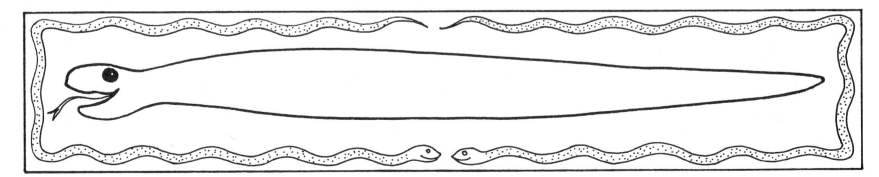

Make this baseboard longer than the longest snake.

Collecting raindrops

What you need
A baseboard (see page 98),
2 large identical jars,
a selection of pots,
2 umbrella counters (different colours),
blue/green rice raindrops,
a 1–6 die.

How to play
Each player takes a large jar, then selects a pot which he places at his side. Players take turns to throw the die and progress up the clouds using their umbrella counters.

When a player reaches the rainbow, he fills his pot with rice raindrops and then pours these into his large jar. The used pot is then put to one side and a new pot chosen, ready for the next journey up the clouds to the rainbow.

When all the pots have been used the winner is the player with the least amount of 'rain' in his jar, shown by direct comparison.

Notes
Good jars can be made by using plastic squash bottles with the tops cut off. (The bottles with rounded hidden bases are unsuitable.)

To make rice raindrops, put some rice in a shallow bowl, sprinkle it with blue and green food colouring, stir it to make sure all the rice is coloured, then spread it out to dry.

37

Santa's store

What you need
A baseboard (see page 99), 2 felt stockings or socks, 2 Santa's helper markers, a selection of small toys or weighted looped parcels, a balance, a 1–6 die.

How to play
Place either toys or parcels in Santa's store, and the felt stockings beside the stockings on the baseboard. Then place the markers on the baseboard stockings.

The players take turns to throw the die and move their marker towards Santa's store along the bootprints. When a player reaches the store, she chooses and collects a toy or parcel and places it inside her felt stocking. The marker is then returned to the stocking on the baseboard. When all of the toys or parcels have been collected the stockings are put in the balance. The winner is the player with the heavier stocking. Alternatively, the winner could be the player with the lighter stocking.

Notes
When using toys children choose what they like to begin with, while parcels help them to concentrate on the weight, aided by being able to hold the parcels by the loops.

All the parcels should be the same size, but different weights. Washers, stones, nails, buttons, etc, embedded in Plasticine may be used to vary the weight of the parcels.

For Santa's helpers, use a polystyrene ball for the head and a card cone for the body (see figure 1).

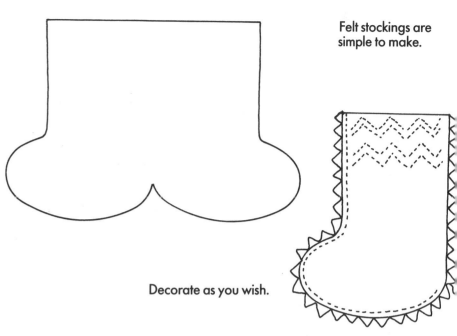

Felt stockings are simple to make.

Decorate as you wish.

Figure 1

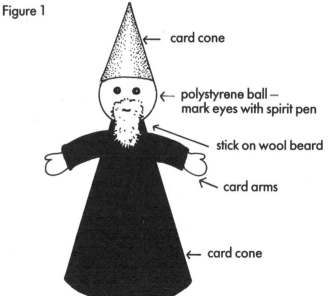

← card cone

← polystyrene ball – mark eyes with spirit pen

← stick on wool beard

← card arms

← card cone

Hide and seek

What you need
2 face baseboards with grids drawn on (see page 99 for grid), enough cards to fill the grid spaces exactly, a 1–6 die.

How to play
Each player has a baseboard. The players take turns to throw the die and collect the number of cards indicated, which are then placed in the spaces on their baseboard. The whole baseboard must be covered to hide the face first, and then the die is thrown to remove the cards and to seek the face. A turn may be split between hiding and seeking: for example, if two spaces are left to cover and a five is thrown, the two spaces may be covered and then three spaces uncovered.

Notes
Children's self-portraits are best for this game. For younger children, a larger grid with fewer spaces can be used.

Beat the clock

For one or two players

What you need
A baseboard (see page 100) divided into 60 equal spaces and marked with 60 spots (each five-spot section is marked by heavier lines), 60 counters to fit over the spots, 12 equal sectors to fit the baseboard, a 1–6 die, a timer.

How to play
This is a game played against the clock. The aim is to fill the baseboard before a set period of time runs out.

The timer is set, then the players take turns to throw the die, pick up the indicated number of counters and place them on the spots. When each five-spot section is filled, a sector is placed over it on the baseboard.

The players beat the clock if all 12 sectors are placed on the baseboard before the set time is up.

Notes
Try setting the timer for ten minutes to begin with. The time can be reduced for more able children and increased for those with less manual dexterity.

Lots of money

What you need
Two worksheets
(copy page 101),
a box of coins,
(1p, 2p, 5p,
10p, 20p and
50p – up to 12
of each coin),
2 dice
(a 1–6 die
and a money die showing the
above coins),
2 pencils.

How to play
The players must throw both dice, reading the number die first and the money die second. For example, if the number die shows 3 and the money die shows 5p, this means the player must pick up three 5p coins and place them on the 5p purse on their sheet. You can only put money on each purse once.

    The players take turns to throw the dice, placing coins, on their purses as they go, and the game ends when a player has money in all six purses.

    When the game is over the coins must be drawn on the purses and the appropriate total value written in the boxes underneath each purse. The overall total could be entered too, depending on the ability of the children. The winner is the first player to fill all six purses or the player with the most money.

Notes
You could use a calculator to find the overall total.

Geometry

'Almost all children find pleasure in working with shape', states Cockcroft, and ideas about shape and pattern are developed from an early age by the exploration of their environment. By helping children to clarify their thoughts and providing accurate mathematical language, teachers will lead children towards a better understanding of shape.

It is important that children have opportunities to explore regular and irregular 3D and 2D shapes, developing an understanding of the properties of shapes by handling and discussing them. A game such as 'Shape family' helps children to think about the properties of certain shapes and to learn their common names.

Positional language is an important aspect of geometry. This may relate to the children themselves, as in PE, to toys such as Big Track or George the Robot, or to 2D pictures such as in the 'Christmas dinner' and 'Where are we?' games.

Moving and fitting together shapes can be experienced in two and three dimensions and children can have great fun studying the packaging of everyday items, examining the way that small boxes fit together within a larger box, for instance.

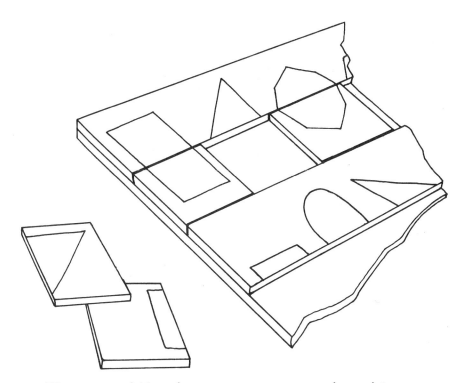

'Shape match' involves symmetry, a popular subject in the primary school. Many children are encouraged to examine reflectional symmetry while rotational symmetry is only mentioned in passing. It is important that we let children create symmetry as well as discover it.

By teaching coordinates through games children learn the skills necessary for graph work and map-reading in a relaxed situation. The coordinates games in this chapter are of two types: in 'The wizard's spell' the coordinates refer to a square on a grid, and in 'Planets' the coordinates describe a point.

Recording may be through art and craft rather than with pencil and paper; children who find great difficulty writing the results of their investigations may derive a great sense of achievement from perhaps 'sewing' a pattern that they have made, or constructing a model.

'Shape match' is for one player only; otherwise all the games are for two players.

The shape family

What you need
2 worksheets (copy page 102), 21 cards with shape attributes, ('triangle', 'three points', 'three sides', 'square', 'four the same length', 'four points', 'rectangle', 'two short sides and two long sides', 'pentagon', 'five points', 'five sides', 'hexagon', 'six sides', 'six points', 'octagon', 'eight sides', 'eight points', 'oval', 'circle', 'round', 'curved'), felt-tipped pens, a 1–6 die.

How to play
Give each player a worksheet, then shuffle the attribute cards and place them face down in a pile.

Players take turns to take a card from the top of the pile and tick the corresponding shape on their worksheet: for example, 'three sides' must be the triangle, and 'curved' could be the circle or the oval. The cards should then be placed face down at the bottom of the pack. If a shape comes up that has already been ticked off, the card is again placed face down at the bottom of the pack and play passes to the other player.

The winner is the first to tick off all eight shapes on their worksheet.

To finish, use the felt-tipped pens to complete the pictures of the shape family.

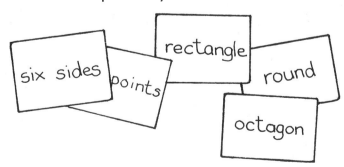

An example of the shape family drawn by a child after playing the game.

Shape match

For one player

What you need
A one-minute sand timer, 3 baseboards (see pages 104–106), 3 sets of cards to go with the baseboards.

How to play
Start with the 'Shape match' board and spread out the cards near it face up. Start the sand timer and, before the sand runs out, try to match the small shape cards to the 'Shape match' board.

The 'Symmetry match' and 'Complete the shapes' boards are played in the same manner against the timer.

The players can compete by improving their own time or by beating other people's times.

Notes
When making the baseboards it is worth making them recessed by using two layers of card and cutting the shapes into the top layer for the matching cards to slot into so that they are not dislodged easily.

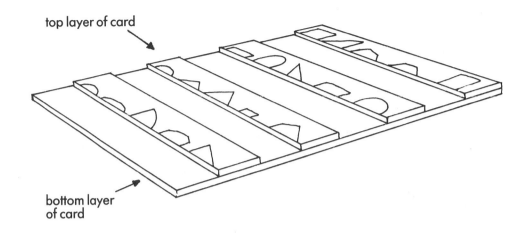

top layer of card

bottom layer of card

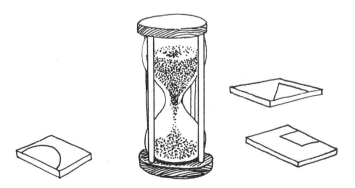

Where are we?

What you need
2 game sheets (copy page 107), pencils.

How to play
Get the children to draw a set of characters along the bottom of the sheet before it is copied. Players decide who will be the instructor and who will follow instructions. They sit back-to-back and the instructor draws a character from the bottom of her sheet on to the castle picture. She describes in detail the position of the character, and the other player has to draw the same character on to his sheet following the instructions given. When all of the characters have been drawn the players compare their sheets to see how closely they match.

By doing this activity several times the players refine their use of positional language.

This is not a game with a winner but an activity where the close co-operation of both players is necessary to achieve good results.

Suggestions for characters to be drawn on the game sheet.

The wizard's spell

What you need
A cauldron board (see page 108)
marked with a 6×6 grid
(numbers along the bottom
written in green,
numbers up the side in red –
written in the spaces,
not on the lines),
2 small cauldron cards,
a number of star cards
to fit in the grid squares,
two 1–6 dice
(one red and one green).

How to play
This is a 'spaces' coordinates game (see introduction to chapter). Before the game begins a number of star cards are placed in some of the spaces on the grid, and each player takes a small cauldron card.

The players take turns to throw the two dice. If a red three and a green two are thrown, for instance, the player finds the appropriate square (two along and three up), takes the star card if there is one there, and places it in their cauldron. If there is no star card in the square, play passes to the other player.

The winner is the player with the higher number of stars on their cauldron and therefore the most 'spell power' at the end of a set time eg ten minutes.

Notes
To make the dice, use red and green coloured spots or spirit pens on blank dice. (Remember to read the X axis before the Y axis).

The children can draw and cut out their own cauldron cards and star cards.

Christmas dinner

What you need
A baseboard,
2 place setting boards
(see page 109),
3 sets of cards
(potatoes, peas, carrots,
chicken, Christmas puddings,
glasses of lemonade),
two 1–6 dice,
2 directional dice
marked 'right', 'left'
'diagonally' (2 of each word),
2 small dolls (such as Duplo dolls)
to use as counters.

lemonade

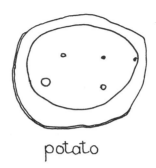

potato

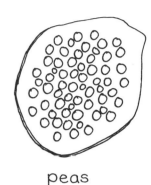

peas

Get the children to illustrate the cards.

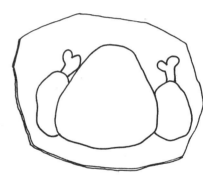

chicken

How to play
Place the dolls on adjacent spaces in the centre of the
baseboard. Put all the items for a Christmas dinner in
spaces on the baseboard – only one item in a space –
and give each player a place setting.

Players take turns to throw the dice and move their
dolls accordingly (number of spaces and direction), if
'diagonally' comes up, the doll may be moved any of the
four diagonal ways.

If a player lands on a space with food or drink on it, he
collects the card and places it on his place setting, (an
item may be collected only once). To win the game a
complete Christmas dinner has to be collected.

Christmas pudding

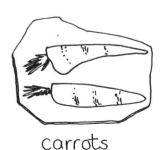

carrots

48

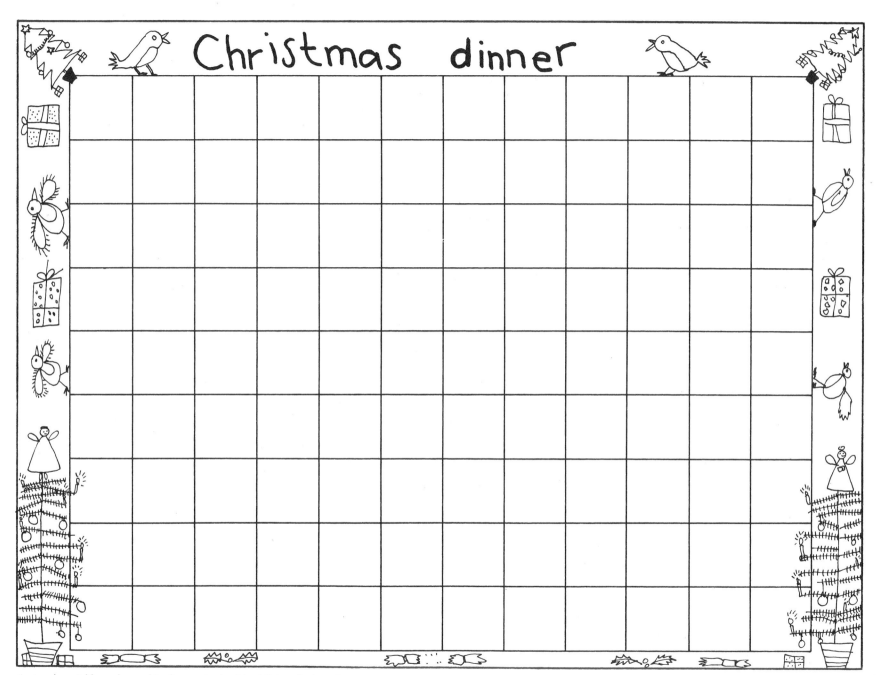

Christmas dinner

A simple grid baseboard is decorated with children's drawings.

Planets

What you need
A baseboard,
a 1–6 X die,
a 1–6 Y die,
18 small cardboard planets,
2 galaxy base cards
(copy page 110).

How to play
This is an 'intersections' coordinates game (see introduction to chapter). Before the game begins, place the planets on any of the cross-over points of the X and Y lines, and give each player a galaxy base card.

The players take turns to throw the two dice, X and Y. If an X4, Y3 coordinate comes up, for instance, and there is a planet on that intersection, the player can remove the planet and place it on their galaxy card. If there is no planet on that intersection, play passes to the other player.

The winner could be:
• the player with the higher number of planets in their galaxy when all planets have been removed from the baseboard (this could take a long time),
• the first person to collect a set number of planets in their galaxy,
• the player with the higher number of planets in their galaxy at the end of a set playing time.

Notes
With any coordinates game the X axis (along) should be read before the Y axis (up). A mnemonic, such as 'along the corridor and up the stairs' or 'chickens always lay eggs (X) on the ground', could be used.

50

Planets

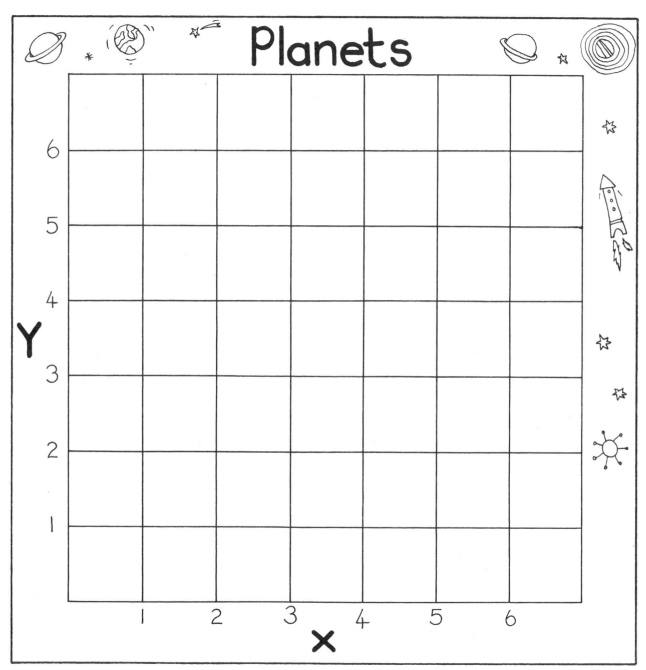

Again a simple grid is illustrated by the children.

Topics and stories

In previous chapters we have grouped games together according to mathematical content. In this chapter we have collected together a few examples of how games may be related to topics, stories and seasonal work.

All the games are suitable for two players.

Winter

Snowflake, snowball, snowman

What you need
A snowman card, 15 snowball cards, 15 snowflake cards, a 0–5 die.

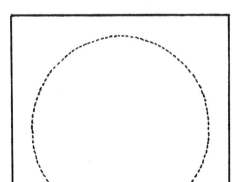

How to play
Players take turns to throw the die and pick up the number of snowflakes indicated by the die. When six or more snowflakes have been collected by a player, six of them may be exchanged for one snowball. The remainder (if there are more than six) may be kept and put towards the next snowball.

The players continue to collect snowballs in this way until one of them wins by collecting six snowballs to exchange for a snowman.

Notes
This game could be played using basic place value boards (see page 111).

A 0–5 die is used to avoid the possibility of directly picking up a snowball. If you use a 1–6 die you will find out if the players realize that they can take a snowball if a six is thrown. (An extra snowflake and snowball card would be needed.)

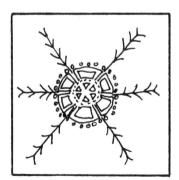

Get the children to make the snowman, snowball and snowflake cards.

Snowman's walk

What you need
A baseboard, a snowman cake decoration, 6 magic beans (see 'Hints and tips' on page 79).

How to play
At the beginning of the game the snowman figure is placed on the snowman picture in the middle of the baseboard. The aim is for one player to 'melt' the snowman by moving him towards the sun, or for the other player to make the snowman bigger by moving him towards the snowflakes. Before the game starts the players decide who will try to make him grow.

The players take turns to throw the magic beans and move the snowman the number of places indicated by the number of beans that fall coloured side up. The snowman is moved to and fro along the track until one player achieves their aim by reaching either the pile of snow or the puddle of water.

The baseboard can be drawn and illustrated by the children.

Spring

Lay, hatch and fly

What you need
Two nest baseboards with ten egg spaces on each (see page 112), 20 egg cards to fit the baseboards (speckled on one side with a baby bird on the other, a 1–6 die.

How to play
Players take turns to throw the die and place the corresponding number of eggs on their nest, speckled side up. When the nest is full of speckled eggs they may be turned over as indicated by the throw of the die to hatch. When all the eggs are hatched the birds are removed as indicated by the die to 'fly away'. The winner is the first player to empty their nest.

A single throw of the die may be split between laying and hatching, or hatching and flying. For example, if there is a space for one more egg to be laid and the player throws a four, the one egg may be laid and three eggs may be hatched.

You could apply the rule that the exact number has to be thrown on the die to finish each stage. The game can be played as three separate but consecutive games, in which case both players have a chance of winning a game.

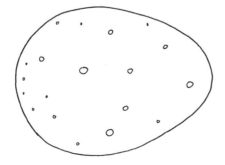

Use an egg-shape on the baseboard as a template for the egg cards, which can be illustrated by the children.

The egg race

What you need
A baseboard, 40 decorated eggs (four each of ten patterns – copy page 113), 2 egg markers.

How to play
This is a variation of pelmanism.

Shuffle the egg cards and place them patterned side down on the table. Players take turns to turn over two eggs: if they match, the player puts them to one side and moves his marker one space along on the board. If the cards do not match they are replaced face down and play passes to the other player. The winner is the first player to reach the bottom of the hill with his egg marker.

Notes
Egg markers in cardboard or tin are available in shops around Easter time (make sure that the bases are flat). Alternatively the children could make their own Easter egg markers using clay which could be decorated and varnished (again make sure that the bases are flat).

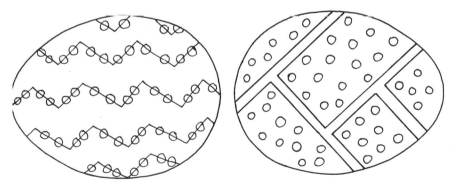

The children can decorate the egg shapes which are then photocopied, mounted on card and cut out.

The Egg Race

start   start   finish   finish

The baseboard is simple for children to make and illustrate.

Summer

Frogging

What you need
A baseboard,
2 small plastic jars
or buckets with
different-coloured
handles,
10 small toy frogs,
5 magic beans.

Children can draw the lily pads
around a pond baseboard,
making sure they are large
enough to take the toy frogs.

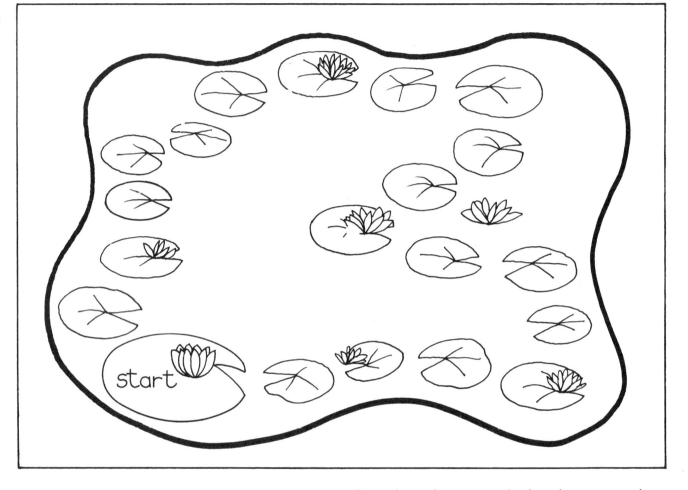

start

How to play
Place the frogs around the pond on the lily pads (only one frog to a pad) and put the jars on the 'start' lily pad.

Players take turns to throw the beans and move their jar from lily pad to lily pad according to the number of beans which land coloured side up. If a player lands on a pad with a frog on it she puts the frog into her jar. Players may move either way round the pond, changing direction between turns but never in the middle of a turn.

When all the frogs have been caught the players match the frogs one to one to see who has more and what the difference is. The player with more frogs wins the game.

Notes
For jar or bucket handles, use coloured pipe-cleaners.

Rubber frogs are available in sorting toy sets; alternatively, draw frogs on to dried butter beans with a green spirit felt-tipped pen.

The rainbow

What you need
An eight-sided die coloured to match the rainbow cards (with one face left blank), 2 sets of rainbow cards (see pages 114 and 115 for templates).

How to play
Players take turns to throw the die and pick up a piece of the rainbow to match the colour shown. If the die shows a blank face or a colour that has already been collected, play passes to the other player.

When all seven colours have been collected the pieces are placed on top of each other in the correct order to make a complete rainbow. The winner is the first player to collect a rainbow.

A more difficult version of the game is to collect the pieces of rainbow in order, starting with the red piece.

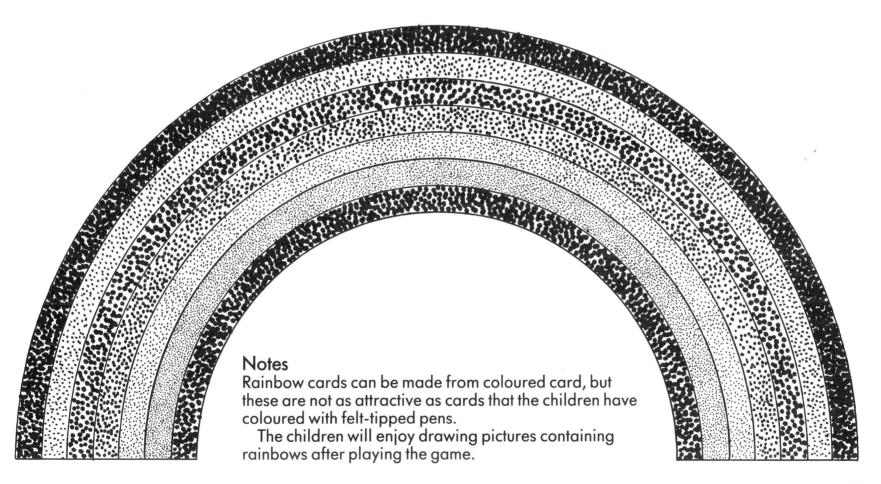

Notes
Rainbow cards can be made from coloured card, but these are not as attractive as cards that the children have coloured with felt-tipped pens.

The children will enjoy drawing pictures containing rainbows after playing the game.

Autumn

Broomsticks

What you need
A selection of card broomsticks of various lengths (see page 116 for templates), a ruler marked in centimetres.

How to play
The players take one broomstick at a time and estimate its length in centimetres (taking turns to make the first estimate). The broomstick is then measured using the ruler, and the player whose estimate is closer keeps the broomstick.

The winner is the player who has most broomsticks when all of them have been measured.

The game can be made more difficult by stating that a player may only keep a broomstick if his estimate is accurate to within one or two centimetres.

Autumn leaves

What you need
2 baseboards
(see pages 117 and 118)
divided into eight
equal sections
and illustrated
with different
half-leaves
(the leaves on each
baseboard should
be different),
16 cards
with the other half
of the leaves
for matching
(see page 119),
8 extra cards
with half-leaves
that do not match
either baseboard
(see page 120).

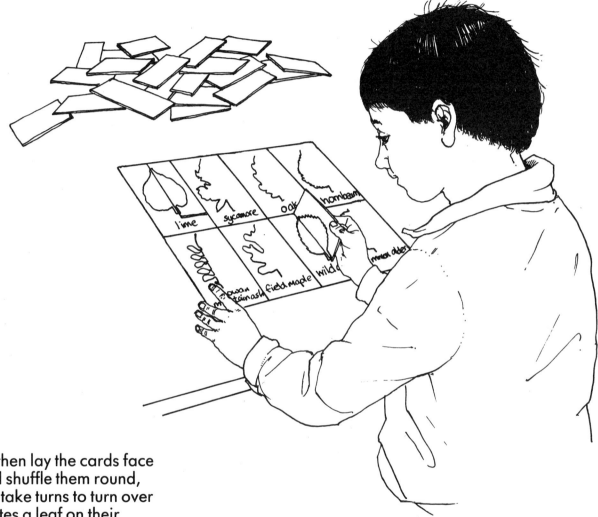

How to play
Give each player a baseboard, then lay the cards face
down on the playing surface and shuffle them round,
mixing them thoroughly. Players take turns to turn over
one card: if the half-leaf completes a leaf on their
baseboard they may place it on the board and complete
the leaf shape; if not, it must be turned face down again
and play passes to the other player.

The winner is the first player to complete all the leaves
on their baseboard.

Christmas

Christmas stockings

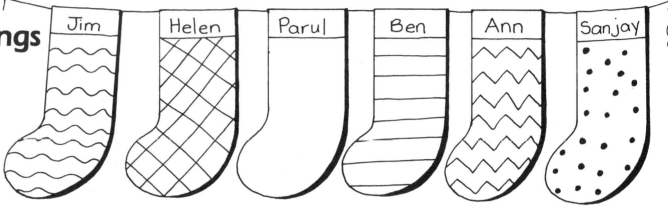

What you need
A die with six patterns,
2 stand-up fireplaces
made of fairly thick card,
12 patterned stockings
(two of each pattern
to match die) –
see page 121 for template.

How to play
Each player has a fireplace baseboard. Players take turns to throw the patterned die, take a stocking which matches the pattern on the die and then hang it on their fireplace.

If the pattern shown on the die is the same as stocking already collected, play passes to the other player.

The winner is the first player to get six different stockings hanging on their fireplace.

Alternatively, you could put names on the tops of the stockings: six names, two of each. Of course a different die would be needed with the initial letters written on. The game would then be played in the same way.

Figure 1

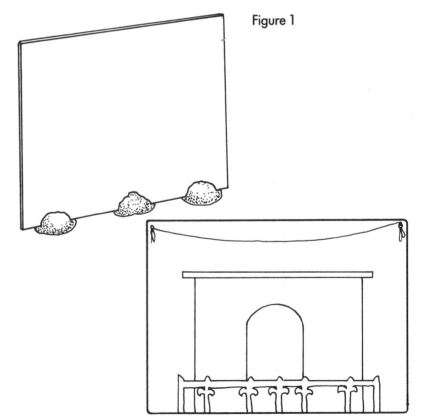

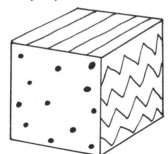

Notes

To make the fireplaces stand up, use a small breakthrough stand or small balls of Plasticine. Tie embroidery thread or wool across the top of the fireplace for the stockings (see figure 1).

To make the stockings, fold pieces of card and draw stocking shapes on them, starting at the fold, and then cut them out (see figure 2).

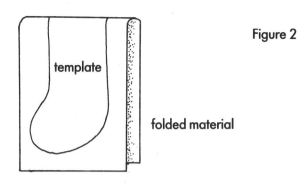

Figure 2

template

folded material

Fill Santa's sleigh

What you need
2 baseboards,
parcel cards
with number bonds
on the back for
2 different numbers
(eg for 6 and 7,
0+6, 1+5 etc,
0+7, 1+6 etc),
bricks to check bonds.

How to play
Give each player a
baseboard, shuffle the
parcel cards and place
them in a pile with
the 'bond' side down.

Each player will collect
parcels for one target
number. Players take turns
to turn over the top
card and work out the
number bond (using
bricks if necessary).
If the answer is the same as their target number they may
place the parcel card in Santa's sleigh on their
baseboard. If the answer is not their target number the
'parcel' is placed to one side.

The winner is the player who has most parcels in their
sleigh when the parcel cards run out.

The players then swap target numbers, shuffle all the
cards, place them in a pile and play again, so it is
possible for each player to win once.

A simple baseboard drawn by children.

Notes
With two different target numbers, the number of
possible bonds for each is different. To make the game
fair, use the same number of parcel cards for each
number by withdrawing some bonds.

To make parcel cards, use metallic card and draw
ribbons with a spirit pen.

Space

Space dara

What you need
A baseboard marked with 30 planets (see page 122), 24 astronauts to fit the baseboard in two different colours.

How to play
'Space dara' is based on a North African game and is played in two parts.

First part
Players take turns to position their 12 astronauts on the board, one at a time. They are not allowed to place more than two of their astronauts adjacent to each other during this part of the game. (This is why there are more planets than astronauts.)

The first part needs much thought and planning because the moves in the second part will depend on how the planets are placed.

Two astronaut cards.

Second part
Players take turns to move their astronauts one space at a time horizontally or vertically, but not diagonally. The aim is to get three astronauts in a row, either horizontally or vertically. When a player achieves this, she can remove one of her opponent's astronauts.

The game is over when one of the players is unable to make any more rows of three, or when all the astronauts belonging to one player have been removed.

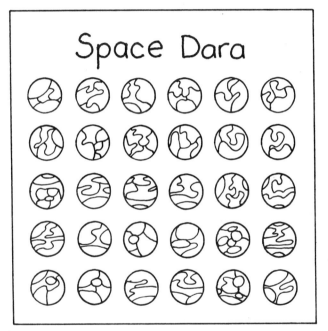

Space Dara

Notes
For young children the game may be played with fewer astronauts, say ten.

Bubble printing is an attractive and speedy way to make the planets, while the astronauts can be made by the children drawing small self-portraits which are then mounted on circles of metallic card (in two colours, one for each player).

Rockets and comets

What you need
A baseboard,
2 Lego spacemen,
a 1–6 die.

Rockets and Comets

100	99	98	97	96	95	94	93	92	91
81	82	83	84	85	86	87	88	89	90
80	79	78	77	76	75	74	73	72	71
61	62	63	64	65	66	67	68	69	70
60	59	58	57	56	55	54	53	52	51
41	42	43	44	45	46	47	48	49	50
40	39	38	37	36	35	34	33	32	31
21	22	23	24	25	26	27	28	29	30
20	19	18	17	16	15	14	13	12	11
Start 1	2	3	4	5	6	7	8	9	10

A simple grid, numbered as shown, is illustrated with rockets and comets, following the same principle as 'Snakes and ladders'.

How to play
Players take turns to throw the die and move the corresponding number of spaces. If a player lands on the tail of a rocket, he can move up the rocket to the number at the nose of the rocket. If he lands on the tail of a comet, he slides down the tail to the number at the star of the comet. Continue in this manner, until one player wins by reaching 100.

Notes
This is, of course, a variation on 'Snakes and ladders', and was made during the recent visit of Halley's comet.

A 1–10 die could be used to speed up the game if your children are impatient.

Birds

Penguins in the snow

What you need
2 baseboards (marked with identical numbers), 2 dice numbered 5 to 10, 20 snowflake cards (plus a few spare).

How to play
Players take turns to throw the two dice. The numbers shown on the dice are added together and the player takes a snowflake card to cover that number on their baseboard. If the number is not shown or is already covered, play passes to the other player.

The winner is the first to cover all the numbers shown on their board with snowflakes.

Notes
The snowflakes cards can be made by sticking snowflake-shaped sequins on to a circle of card that matches the background card. If sequins are not available, use drawings or paper cut-outs.

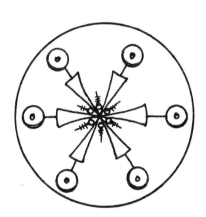

Get the children to draw penguins to illustrate this simple baseboard.

3 2 1 eggs

What you need
A baseboard marked with 18 egg shapes (see page 123), 18 card egg shapes to fit the outlines on the baseboard.

How to play
Players place all the eggs in the nest, decide which player will start the game (see 'Hints and tips' on page 79), then take turns to remove the eggs. They are allowed to remove one, two or three eggs, and they are not allowed to miss a go.

   The player who removes the last egg from the nest is the loser.

Notes
The egg-shaped cards can be decorated to represent a wild bird's egg, such as a blackbird's – pale blue with brown speckles.

Use an egg on the baseboard as a template for the egg cards.

Stories

Sleepy sheep

What you need
2 bed folders with pockets for the sheep, 20 cardboard sheep (ten outlined in red and ten outlined in blue), 20 sheep cards, 20 plain cards.

How to play
This game originated after reading *Ten Sleepy Sheep* (Hippo Books).

   Each player has a bed folder with ten sheep of one colour in the storage pocket at the left-hand side of the bed. These folders stand as shown in the illustration. Spread out the 20 sheep cards and the 20 plain cards face down and shuffle them thoroughly.

   Players take turns to turn over two cards. If a player turns up two sheep cards, these are removed and placed to one side, and the player can put two sheep to bed in the right-hand side of their folder. If one sheep card and one plain card, or two plain cards are turned up, they must be turned back over and play is passed to the other player. The winner is the player who gets ten sheep into bed first.

sleepy sheep

sheep card

Notes
To make folders, see diagrams. Do not make the pockets too deep or it will be difficult to get the sheep out again.

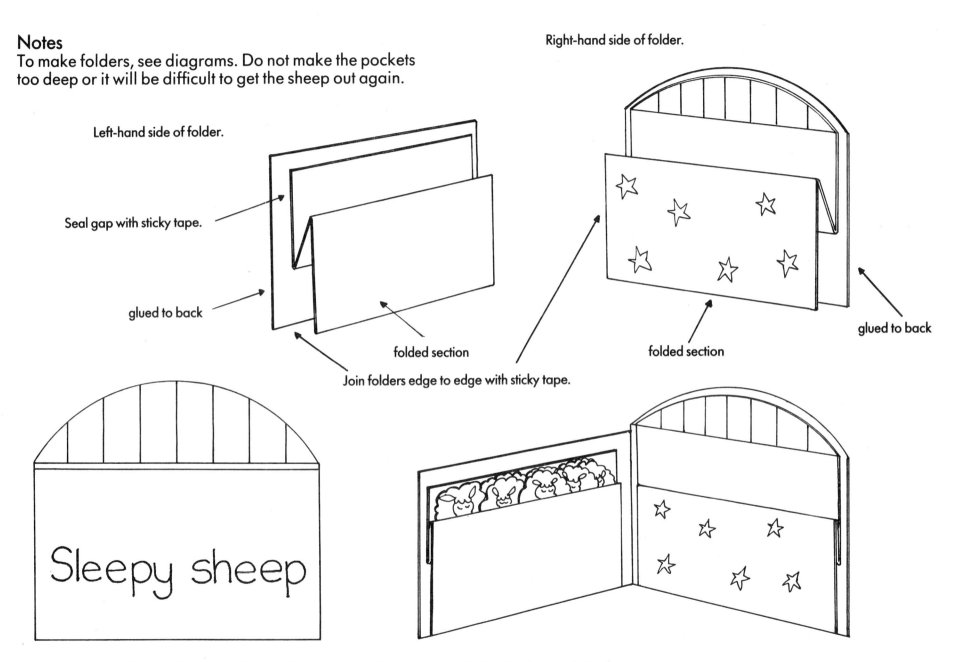

Left-hand side of folder.

Right-hand side of folder.

Seal gap with sticky tape.

glued to back

folded section

glued to back

folded section

Join folders edge to edge with sticky tape.

Closed sleepy sheep folder when both sides have been stuck together.

Sleepy sheep

Folder standing ready to play.

The enormous turnip

What you need
A baseboard, 2 sets of standing characters, 2 packs of 0–5 cards (number words), a copy of *The Great Big Enormous Turnip* by Alexei Tolstoy and Helen Oxenburg (Heinemann/Pan).

Standing characters, made by the children.

How to play
The characters must travel around the turnip field in the correct order according to the story. Shuffle the cards and place them face down on the playing area. In turn, players take a card from the top of the pile, move a character according to the number on the card, then place the card face down at the bottom of the pack. The old man must be the first character to be moved, followed in order by the others.

You may, if you wish, have more than one character on the move by splitting the number on the card: for example, if a player turns up a four card, they can share it between two characters, perhaps moving one character one space and the other three spaces.

Continue in this manner, moving all the characters into position on the board.

If a character lands on the pond space, they unfortunately have to go to the Enormous Turnip via the pond, following the arrows which lead around the pond and then back on to the correct track.

The winner is the player who gets all the characters into position first.

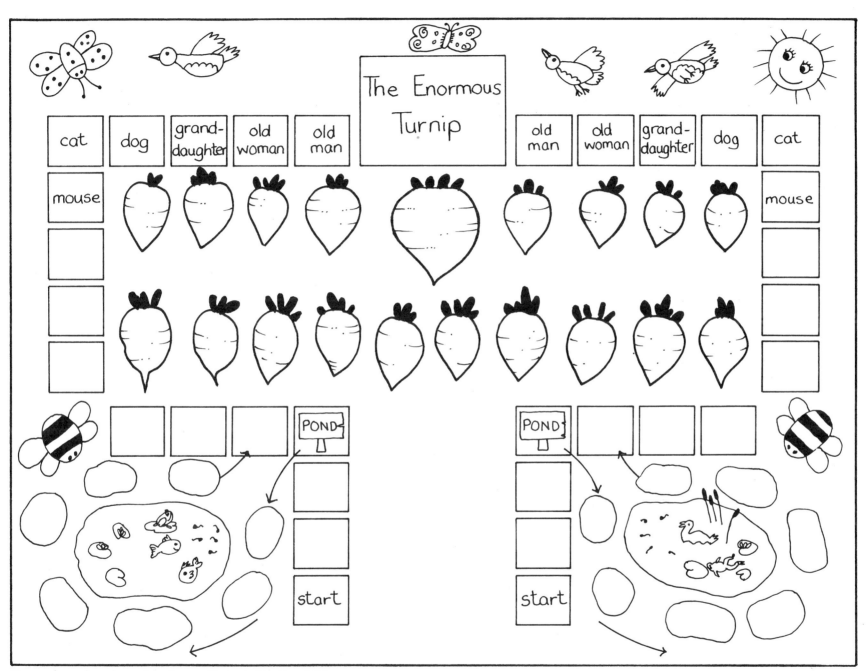

cat	dog	grand-daughter	old woman	old man	**The Enormous Turnip**	old man	old woman	grand-daughter	dog	cat
mouse										mouse

POND

POND

start

start

Draw a large baseboard as shown, illustrated by the children.

Bear on the stairs

What you need
A baseboard (see page 124), a bear character, a 1–6 die, a copy of *Hairy Bear* ed Pam Hutchinson (Arnold Wheaton).

How to play
To begin the game, the bear character is placed on the middle stair of the staircase. One player tries to move the bear up to the top stair and back to bed, while the other tries to move him to the bottom stair where he will discover his cubs having a midnight feast. The players takes turns to throw the die and the bear is moved up and down the stairs according to the number thrown, until one player achieves her aim.

The bear character can be fixed to a Unifix cube, secured with Plasticine.

Notes
Each step on the stairs should be big enough to accommodate the base of the bear character to avoid confusion. Make sure that there is an equal number of stairs above and below the central stair.

Sunflower game

What you need
A number of 'stem' cards with various lengths of stem and various leaf arrangements, 2 identical flower cards (see page 125), 12 magic beans (see 'Hints and tips'), a copy of *The Sunflower that Went FLOP* ed Pam Hutchinson (Arnold Wheaton).

How to play
Players sit at a straight-edged table so that there is plenty of 'growing space' for their sunflower. Each player takes a flower card and places it at the edge of the table in front of him, while the stem cards are placed on one side, face up.

   The players take six magic beans each and throw them. They match any that have fallen painted-side up to see who has more painted sides showing. This player selects a stem card, which is then used to make the player's flower 'grow' away from the edge of the table. This is repeated until all the stem cards have been chosen. The winner is the player whose sunflower has grown the most.

Notes
In order to compare the flowers accurately, the base of the stems must be in the same position – this is why the edge of the table is useful. Obviously no gaps should be left between the cards that make up the plant.

   To ensure that all the stem parts join up accurately, draw one very long stem on a piece of card and then cut it into many shorter lengths, or use the template on page 125 to make up various stem lengths.

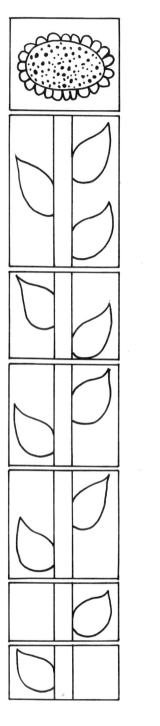

Bad baby game

What you need
2 baseboards, 2 elephant and bad baby figures, 2 sets of card characters, 2 sets of cards marked 1st to 7th in figures, 2 sets of cards marked first to seventh in words, 4 tea-time cards, a copy of *The Elephant and the Bad Baby* by Alfrida Vipont and Raymond Briggs (Hamish Hamilton/Penguin).

the elephant and the bad baby

How to play
Shuffle the cards and place them face downwards. Each player takes a baseboard and places an elephant and bad baby on the left-hand side where marked.

The players take turns to turn over the top playing card. If '1st' is turned over, the player may place the ice-cream man on his baseboard. The card is then placed at the bottom of the pile and play goes to the other player. If the card turned over does not show the next ordinal number, it is placed at the bottom of the pile and play goes to the next player.

The winner is the first player to fill their baseboard and then turn over a 'tea-time' card.

| first | second | third | fourth |

the elephant and the bad baby · the ice-cream man · the pork butcher · the baker · the snack

Make the baseboard large enough to accommodate the children's cards.

74

the ice-cream man

the pork butcher

the grocer

the snack bar man

the baker

the lady from
the sweet shop

the barrow boy

fifth   sixth   seventh   rumpeta rumpeta rumpeta

ar man · the grocer · the lady from the sweet shop · the barrow boy · all down the road ·

Dinosaurs and cabbages

What you need
A field baseboard marked with an 8×8 grid, enough 'cabbages' to fill the baseboard grid and made to fit the squares, 2 dinosaur cards on which to place 'eaten' cabbages, a 0–6 die.

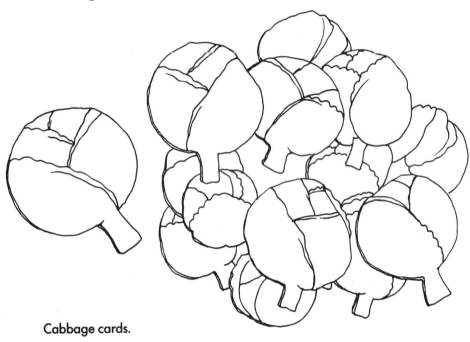

Cabbage cards.

How to play
The players place one cabbage in each square of the field baseboard, then take turns to throw the die to determine how many cabbages their dinosaur eats. This number of cabbages is taken from the field and placed on their dinosaur card. When all the cabbages have been 'eaten' the players match their cabbages, one to one; the player with more cabbages is the winner.

Notes
This game can be simplified for younger or less able children by drawing a smaller grid and using fewer cabbages. (We drew grids of different sizes on the front and back of our baseboard card.)

If you can obtain small dinosaur models the children enjoy using them to visit the field and gobble up the cabbages.

Dinosaur cards.

A simple grid decorated by the children.

Hints and tips

How to start a game

There are many ways to decide who starts a game; here are just a few.

For two players
Coin
A coin can be flipped by one player and covered until the other player calls 'heads' or 'tails'. If the call is correct, the caller begins the game; if not, the player who flipped the coin begins.

Fingers
Two players place a hand behind their backs. On the count of three they show their hands with any number of fingers extended, at the same time calling 'odds' or 'evens'. The player who guesses correctly starts the game (this may need to be repeated).

For two or more players
Dice
A favourite way to decide order of play is for all players to throw a die – the highest throw starts the game. The order of play may be clockwise from the highest score, or from highest to lowest throws of the die.

Sticks
A number of sticks or straws equivalent to the number of players are held by one player so that they appear to be of uniform lengths, although one stick or straw should be shorter than the rest. The players choose one each – the player with the short stick or straw starts the game.

 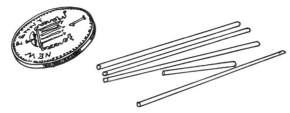

Progressing along a track game

Beans
Magic beans are butter beans painted on one side (lead-free car paint works well). A player takes a set number (usually six) in their hand, shakes the beans and drops them on to the area of play. The number of beans that land coloured side up indicates the number of moves to be made.

Very young children find beans easier to use than a die as they can move the beans to one side as they count them.

Dice and spinners
Ways of using dice have already been discussed in the Introduction. Many types of dice are available. Large foam dice may be suitable for young children or in classes where dice go missing. Smaller foam dice may be suitable for older children where the noise of throwing dice is a problem. The noise problem may be lessened when using ordinary dice by throwing them on to a carpet tile or small piece of carpet.

Although six-sided dice are the most common, dice are available with other numbers of sides, say four, eight, ten or twelve. We have found ten-sided dice marked with the numerals 0–9 to be very useful, especially for place value games. These are available from educational suppliers such as E J Arnold, who also supply blank six-sided dice. Blank dice can be written or drawn on to suit the needs of a particular game. If you have a limited supply of dice you can change what is shown on the faces by covering them with sticky spots which can be written on.

Spinners, also available from educational suppliers, provide a change from dice.

Cards

Blank playing cards are useful for a variety of games as you can write or draw on them to suit your game. They are available from educational suppliers, with either two blank sides or one blank side and one decorated side.

Duplicating

If a game requires more than one set of identical pieces there are several short-cuts to reproduce them. If you are drawing on paper, hold the original picture up to a window and trace it on to another sheet of paper. A photocopier can be used when the drawing is still in outline form to be coloured in afterwards. Photocopiers are also very useful for enlarging or reducing.

The photocopiable section (pages 82 to 125) may be useful when making your games, bearing in mind that children should be encouraged to make and illustrate the games as far as possible.

Mistakes

Do not despair if a small mistake is made when illustrating or assembling a game. If the game is on white card, correction fluid can be used. If you are using coloured card, a small patch of the same coloured card can be placed over the mistake.

Covering

The life of games can be extended by covering them with protective film. This could be a clear plastic bag or sticky-backed plastic, but the most effective and professional-looking finish available to teachers is to laminate them. Some schools are lucky enough to have their own laminator. Alternatively, you may find one at your local teachers' centre. Make sure that the games are narrow enough to be fed through the laminator.

Storage

Games are less likely to be played if they are difficult for the children to get out, so they must be easily accessible. Well-planned storage also lessens the likelihood of games being damaged or lost.

Make sure labels are clear and visible, and remember that there is little point in putting them on the tops of boxes if they are to be stacked. If there is more than one container for a game it is sensible to label them in a similar way. A label that includes a small picture makes recognition easier for young children and quicker for older children and adults. Spirit pens can be used to write and draw on plastic containers.

Different types of games require different types of storage. Here are a few of the types that we have found most useful.

Cardboard boxes
Available in various sizes, we found the most useful were those to fit A4 and A5 papers, and playing-card size.

Plastic boxes
Available in various sizes, depths and colours.

Plastic zipped envelopes
Available in various sizes.

Corrugated plastic portfolios
Available in various sizes, these are invaluable for storing baseboards, and are more accessible to young children than drawers in a plan chest.

All of the above are available from educational suppliers, such as E J Arnold, Parkside Lane, Dewsbury Road, Leeds LS11 5TD. The plastic portfolios can also be purchased from art shops.

Bibliography

Child Education magazines (Scholastic Publications Ltd).
Games of the World F V Grunfeld (UNICEF).
Mathematics 5–11 (HMSO).
Mathematics Counts Dr W H Cockcroft (HMSO).
Count Me in (ILEA Learning Resources Branch).
40 Maths Games to Make and Play M Williams and H Somerwill (Macmillan Education).
Workjobs 1 and *2* ed M B Lorton (Addison-Wesley).
Mathematics Their Way ed M B Lorton (Addison-Wesley).
Primary Mathematics Today E M Williams and H Shuard (Longman).
Working with Number Lines (ILEA Learning Resources Branch).
The Elephant and the Bad Baby A Vipont and R Briggs (Hamish Hamilton/Penguin).
The Great Big Enormous Turnip A Tolstoy and H Oxenbury (Heinemann/Pan).
Hairy Bear ed P Hutchinson (Arnold Wheaton).
Meg's Veg H Nicoll and J Pieṅkowski (Heinemann/Penguin).
The Sunflower that went FLOP ed P Hutchinson (Arnold Wheaton).
Three Squeaky Dragons U Daniels and J Coop (Granda Television *Let's Go Maths* series).

Reproducible material

Notes

Many of the following pages are suitable for reproduction without any alteration of size. Pictures of baseboards are to scale and are intended to be used to stimulate children to produce their own illustrations for the games.

Dimensions of the games have not been given as most games can be made as large or as small as you wish. Size may be related to the age of the children using the games, storage, or the size of cardboard available. However, it is necessary to keep playing pieces in proportion to the size of the baseboard.

Baseboard for 'The posting game', see page 8

84

Templates for 'Weather sets', see page 10

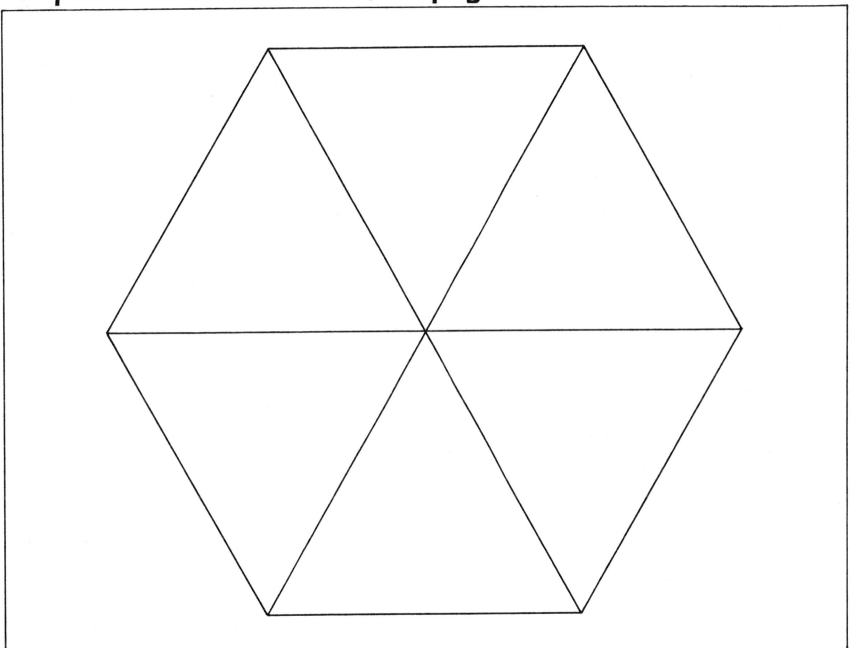

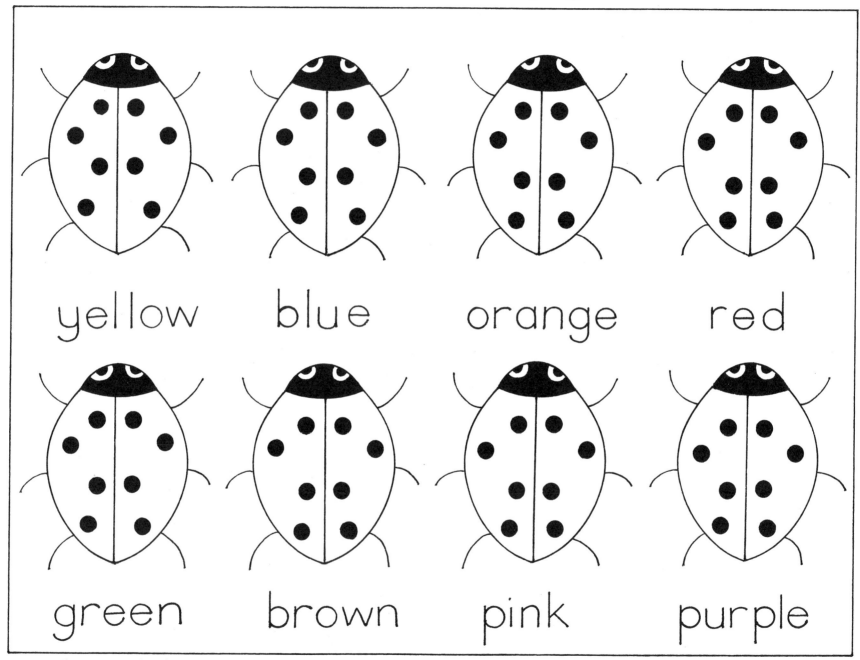

yellow   blue   orange   red

green   brown   pink   purple

Baseboard for 'Mix a spell', see page 14

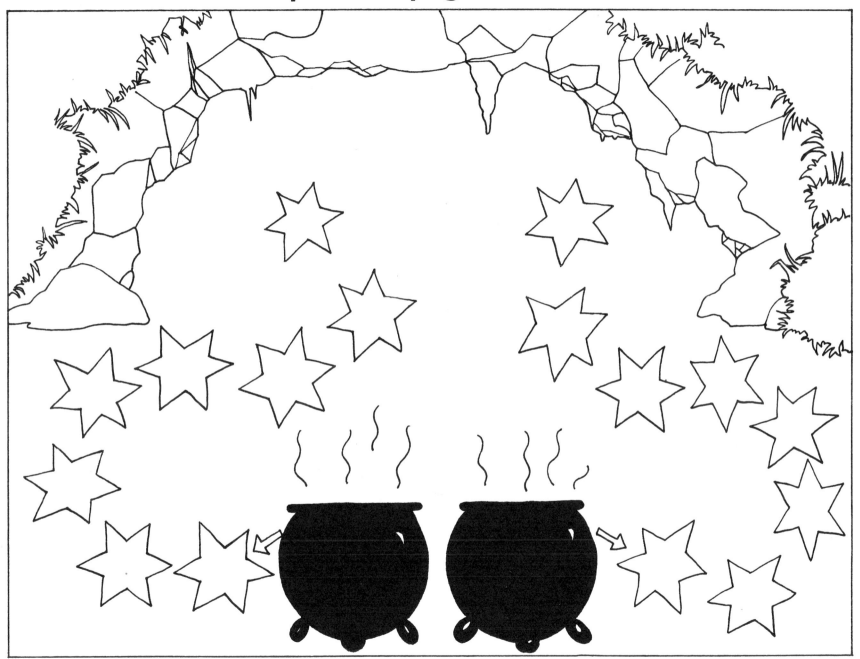

Worksheet for 'Hungry frog', see page 15

Baseboard for 'Traffic wardens', see page 16

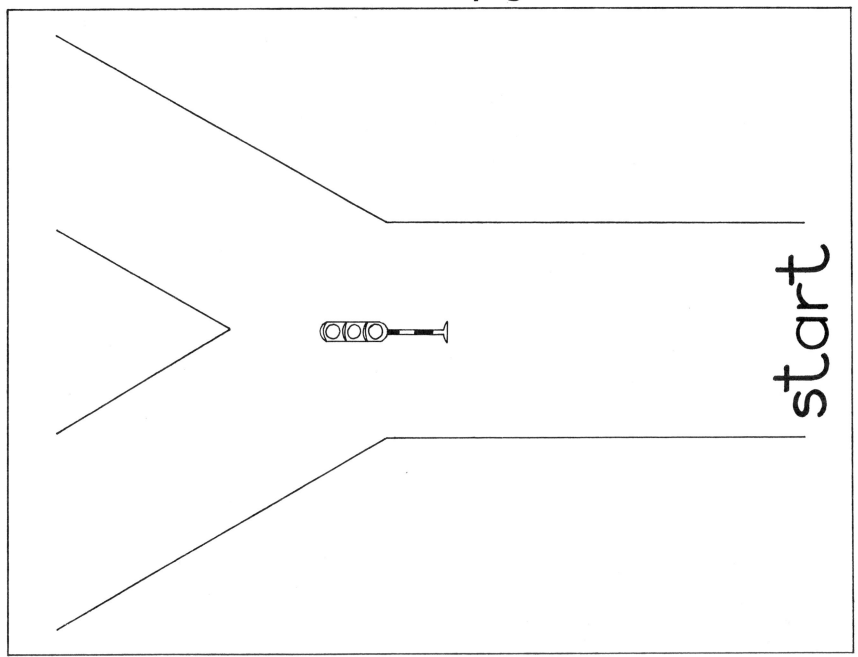

start

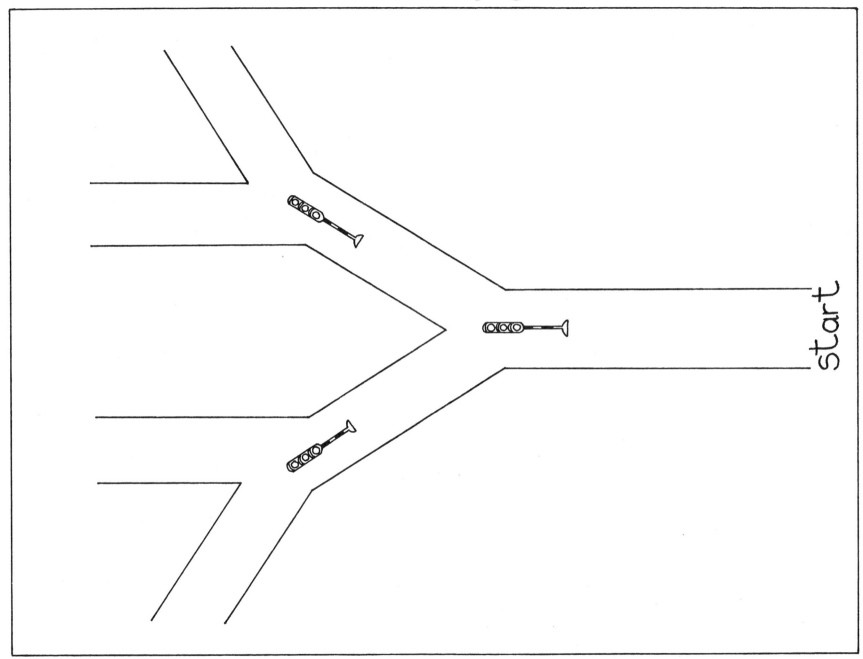

start

Baseboard for 'Hopscotch', see page 23

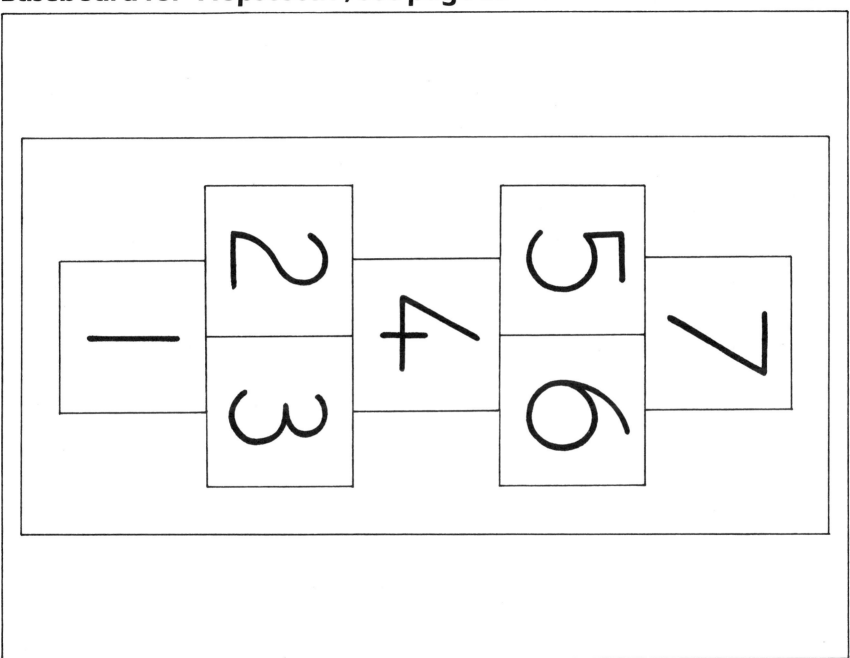

Cards for 'Building site', see page 26

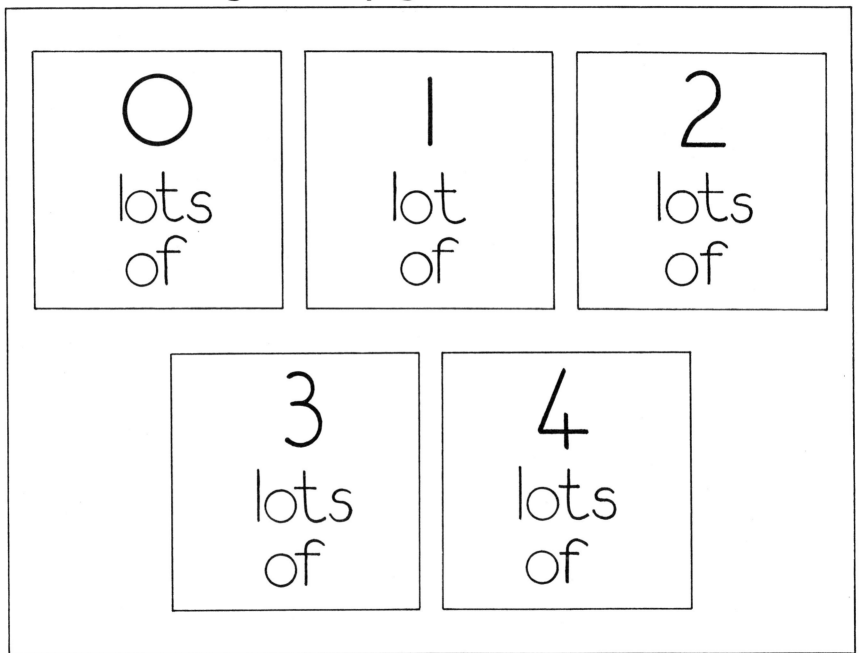

Baseboard for 'Building site', see page 26

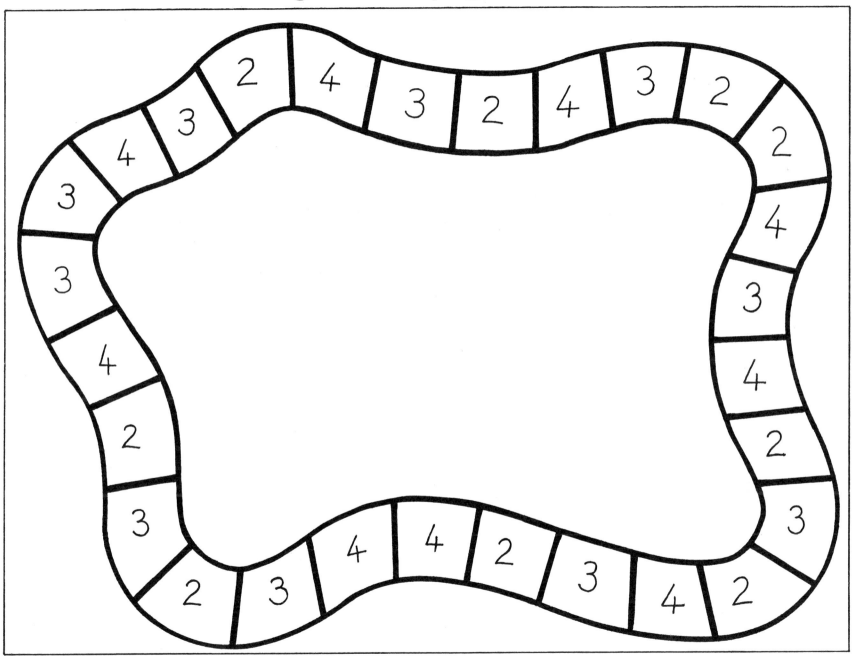

bunches	flowers

Baseboard for 'Dogs and bones', see page 30

Baseboard for 'Ladybird family', see page 31

ladybird family	ladybirds	spots

This page may be photocopied for use in the classroom and should not be declared in any return in respect of any photocopying licence.

Templates for 'Longest line', see page 35

Baseboard for 'Collecting raindrops', see page 37

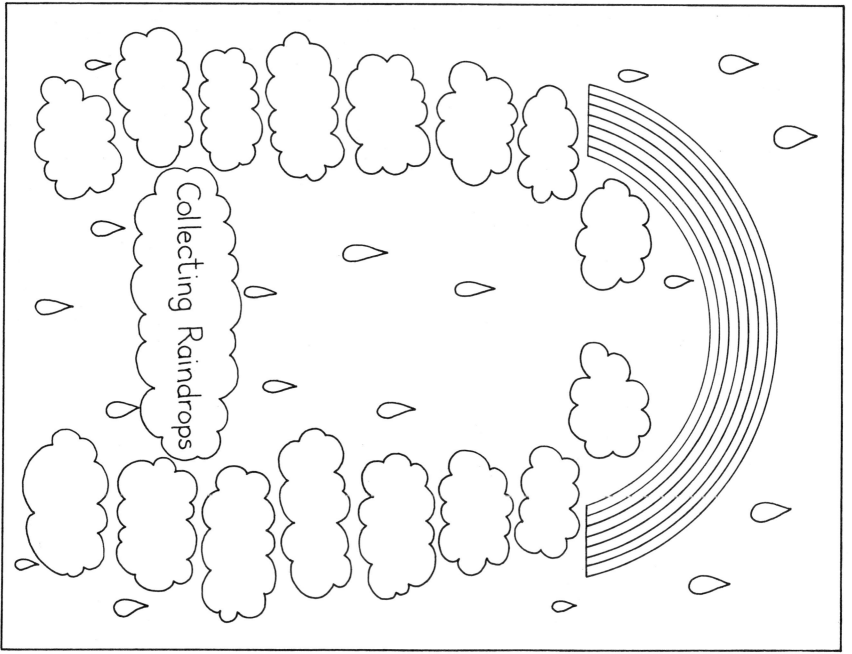

Collecting Raindrops

Baseboard for 'Santa's store', see page 38

Template for 'Beat the clock' baseboard, see page 40

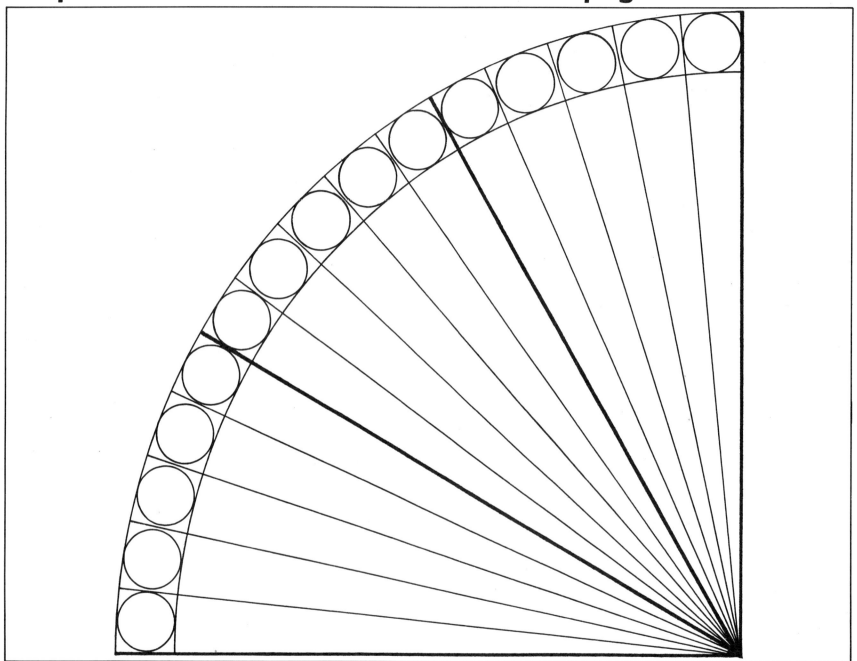

Worksheet for 'Lots of money', see page 41

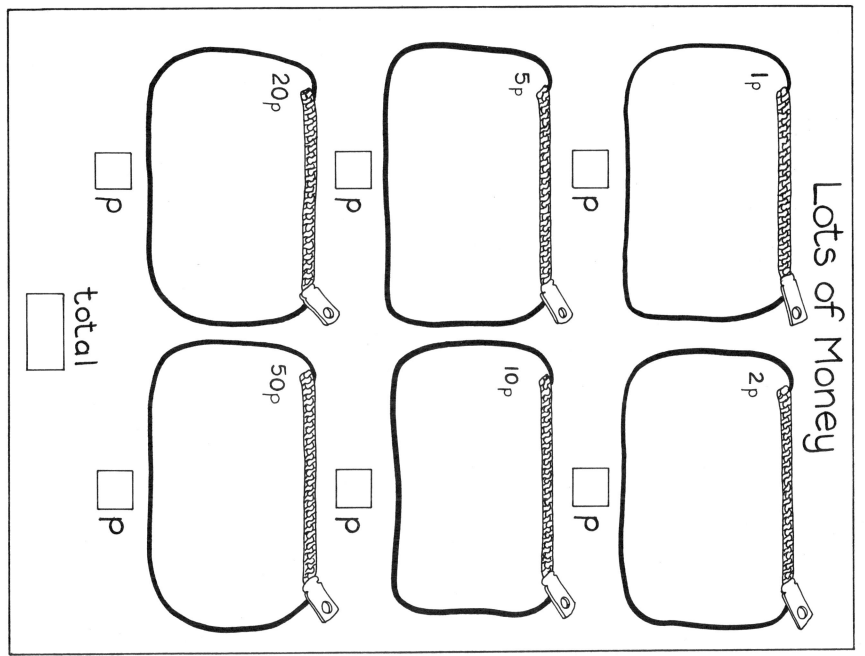

Lots of Money

20p ☐ p

5p ☐ p

1p ☐ p

50p ☐ p

10p ☐ p

2p ☐ p

total ☐

Worksheet for 'The shape family', see page 44

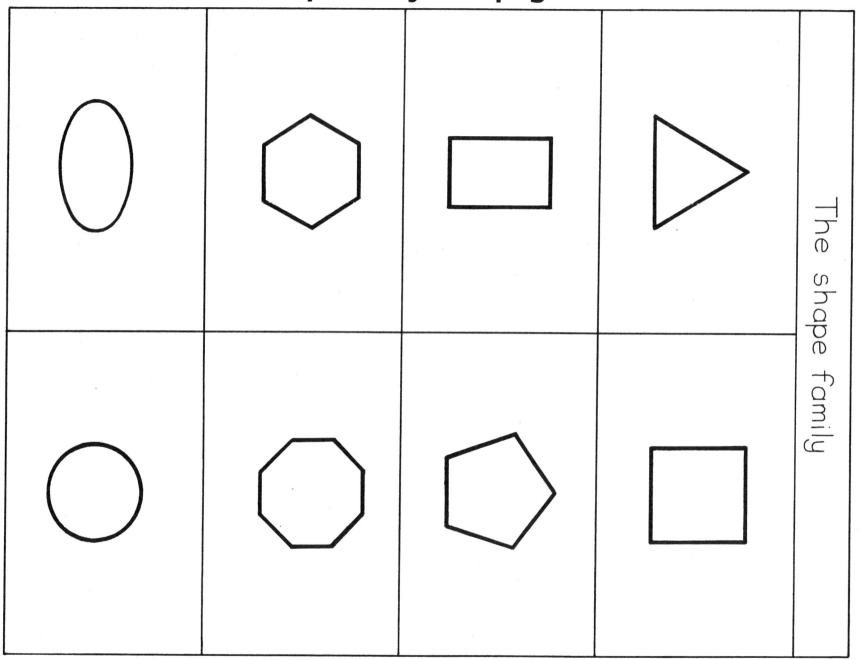

The shape family

Baseboard for 'Shape match', see page 45

Baseboard for 'Symmetry match', see page 45

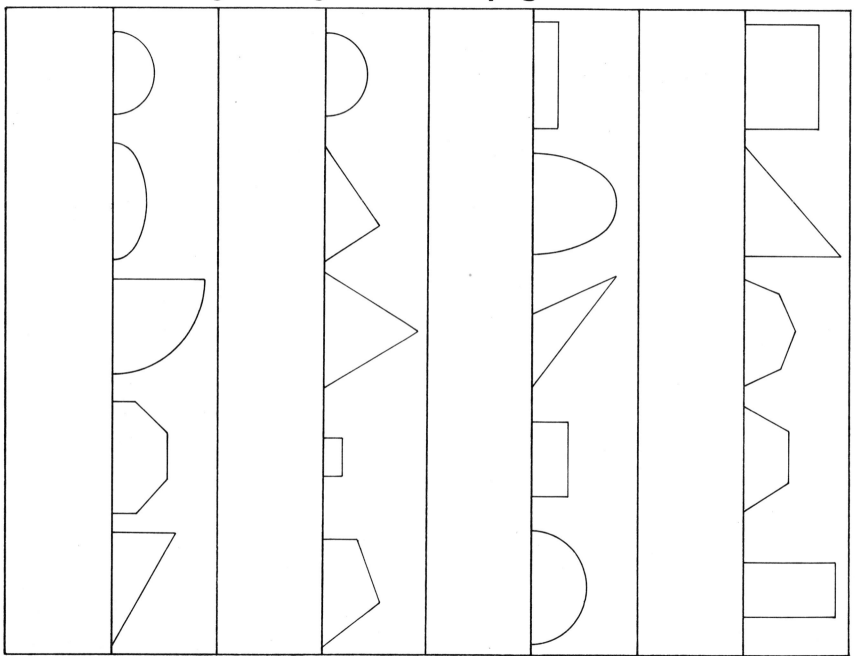

Baseboard for 'Complete the shapes', see page 45

Baseboard for 'Complete the shapes', see page 45

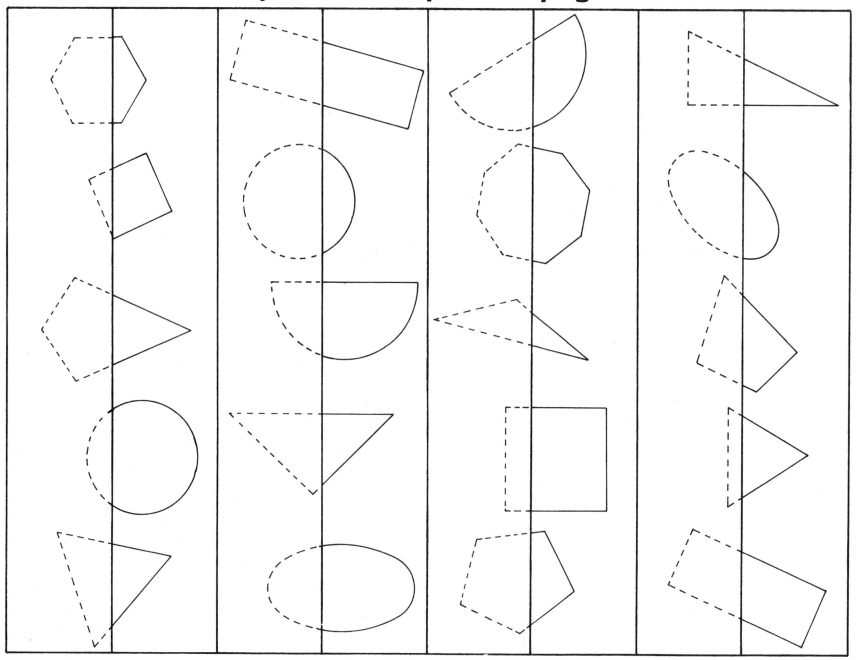

Baseboard for 'Where are we?', see page 46

Baseboard for 'The wizard's spell', see page 47

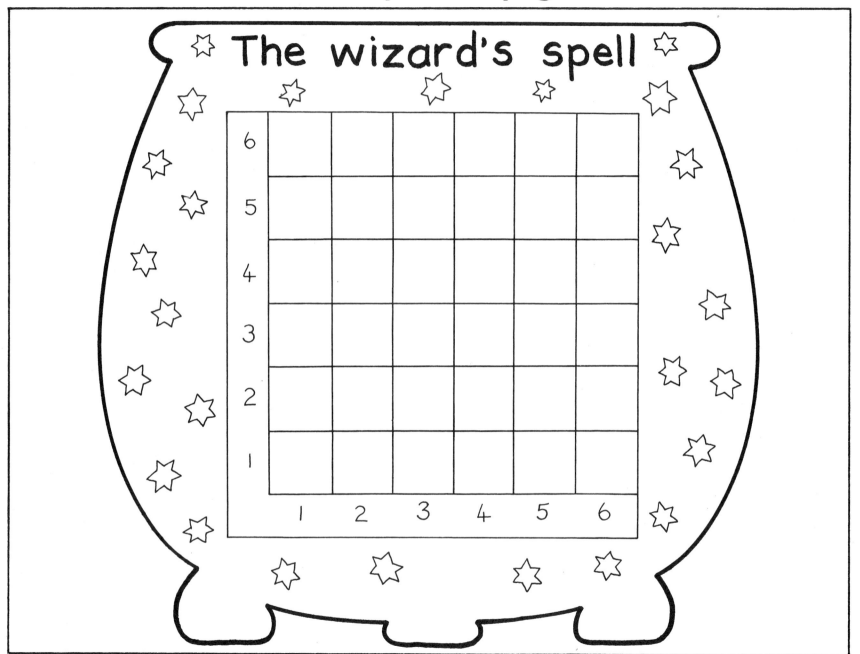

Place setting board for 'Christmas dinner', see page 48

Galaxy base card for 'Planets', see page 50

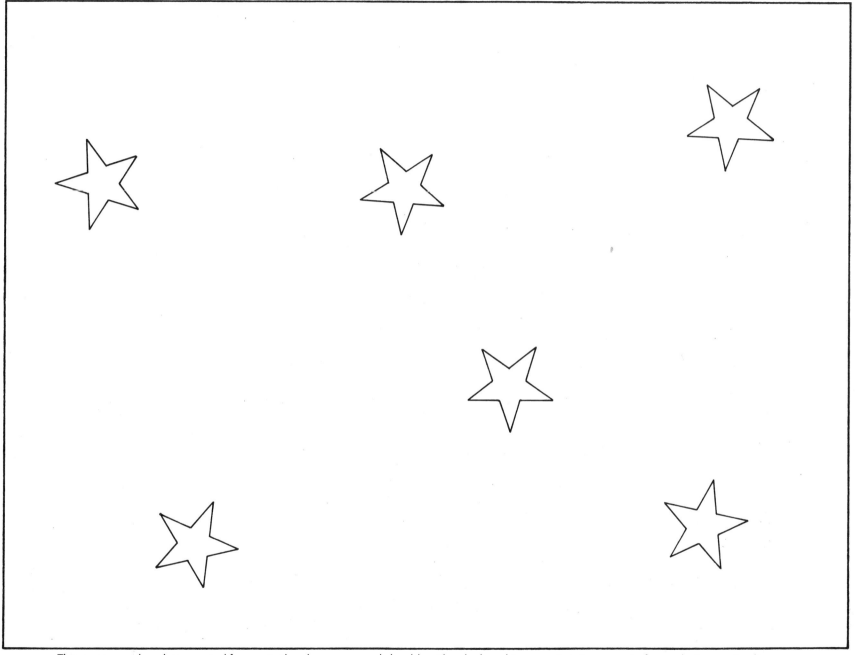

Place value baseboard, see page 53

Baseboard for 'Lay, hatch and fly', see page 55

Egg shapes for 'The egg race', see page 56

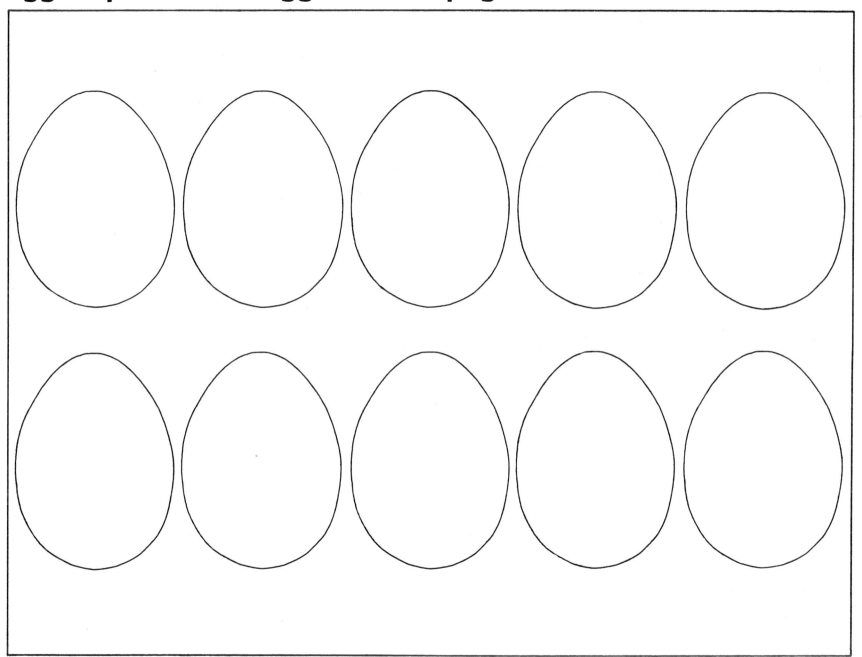

Templates for 'The rainbow', see page 59

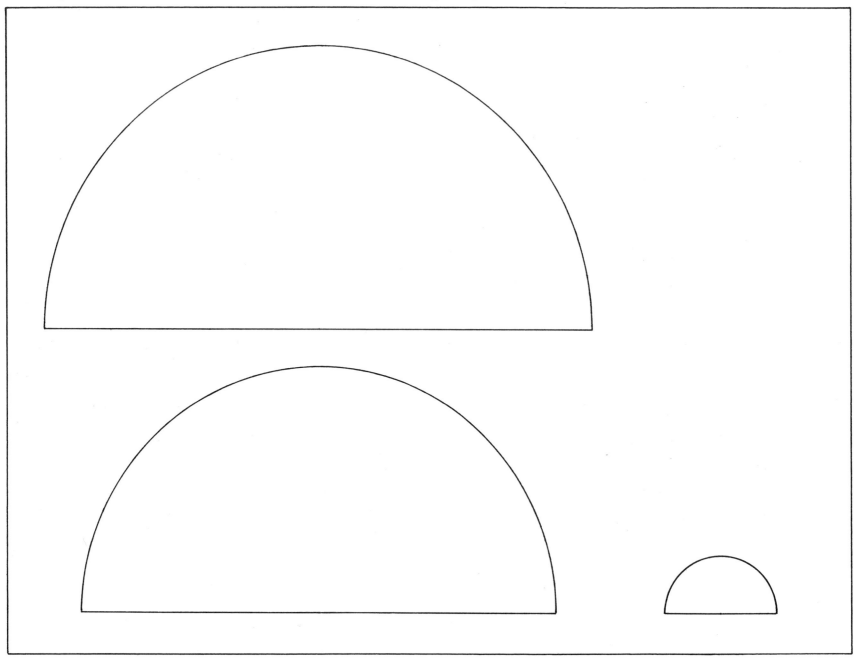

Templates for 'The rainbow', see page 59

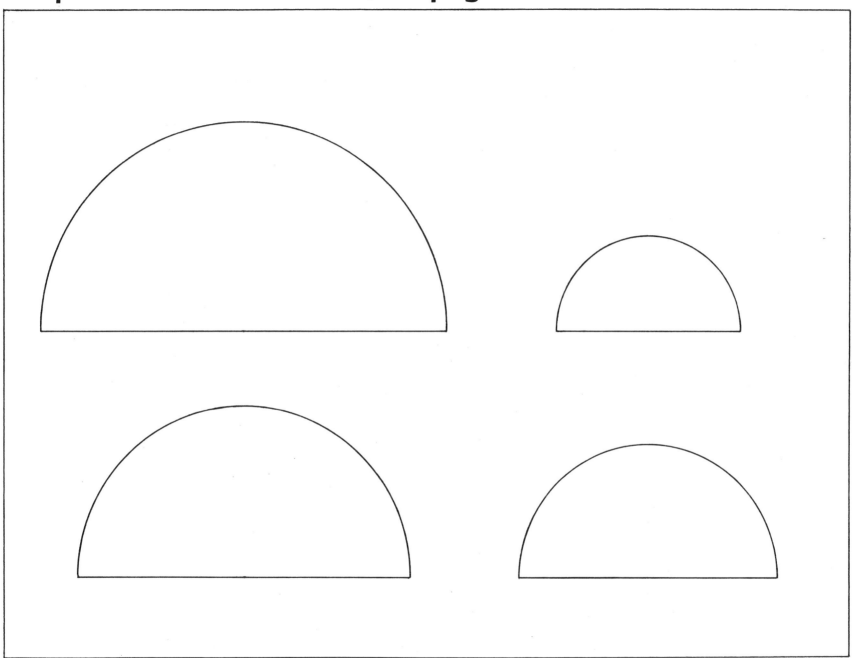

Templates for 'Broomsticks', see page 60

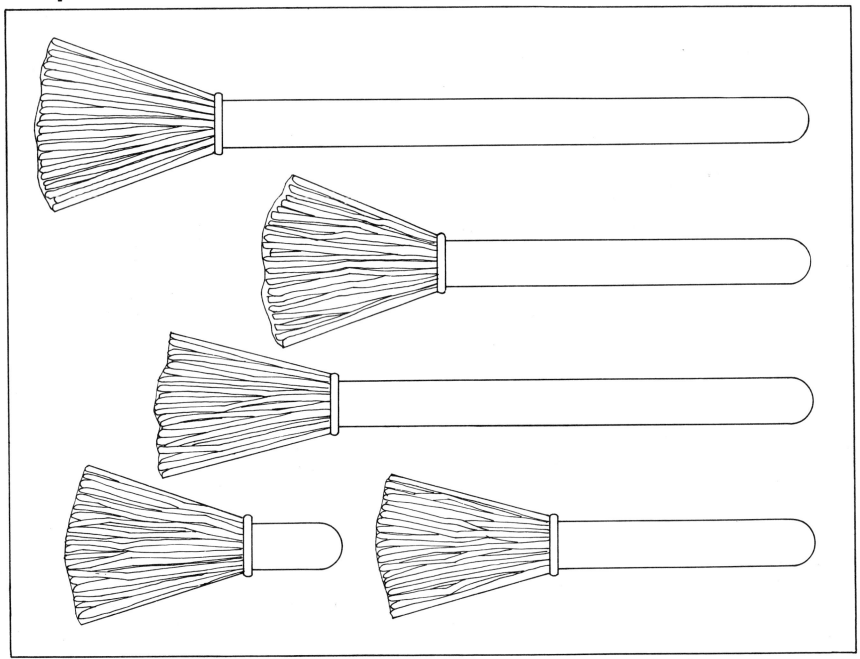

Baseboard for 'Autumn leaves', see page 61

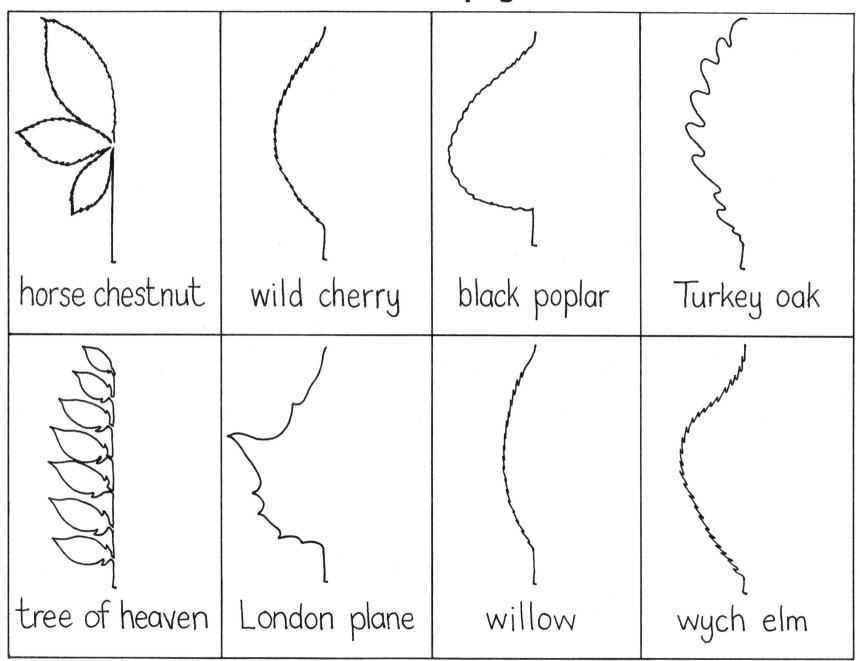

| horse chestnut | wild cherry | black poplar | Turkey oak |
| tree of heaven | London plane | willow | wych elm |

Baseboard for 'Autumn leaves', see page 61

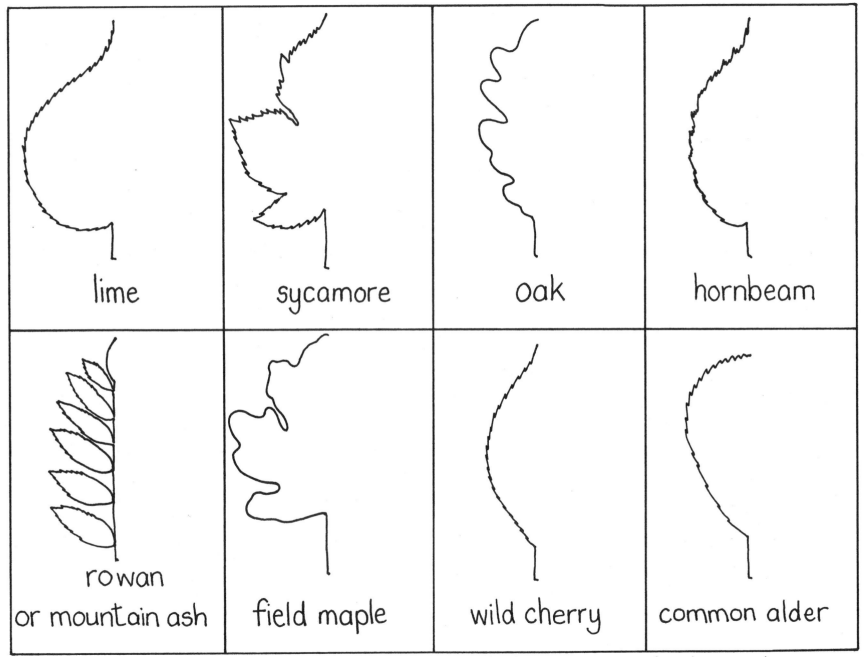

lime

sycamore

oak

hornbeam

rowan
or mountain ash

field maple

wild cherry

common alder

Cards for 'Autumn leaves', see page 61

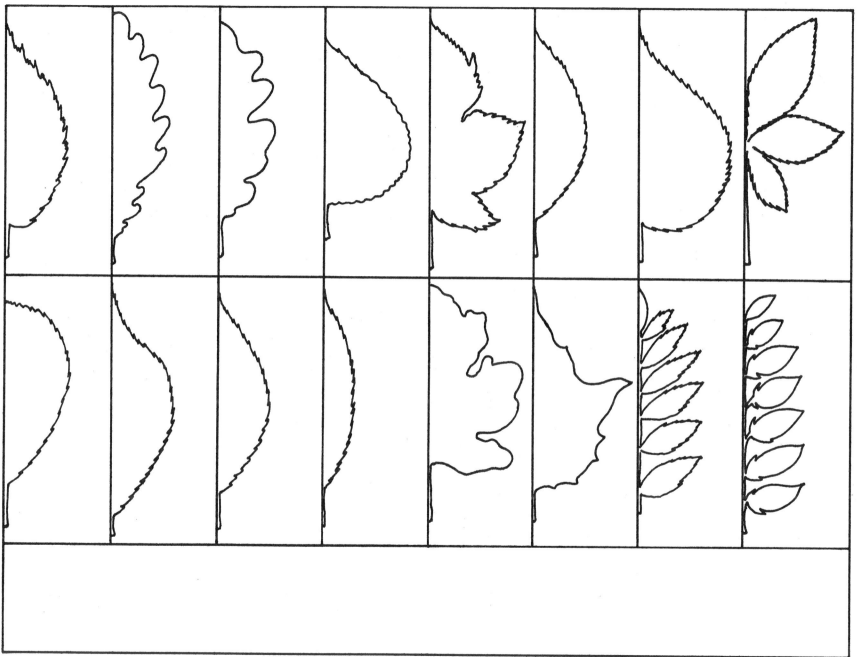

Cards for 'Autumn leaves', see page 61

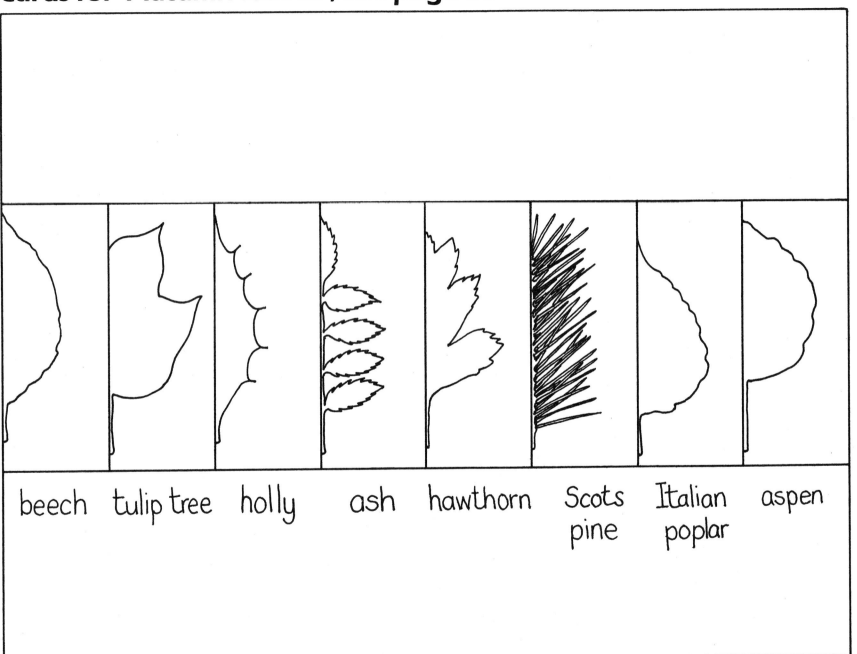

beech · tulip tree · holly · ash · hawthorn · Scots pine · Italian poplar · aspen

Template for 'Christmas stockings', see page 63

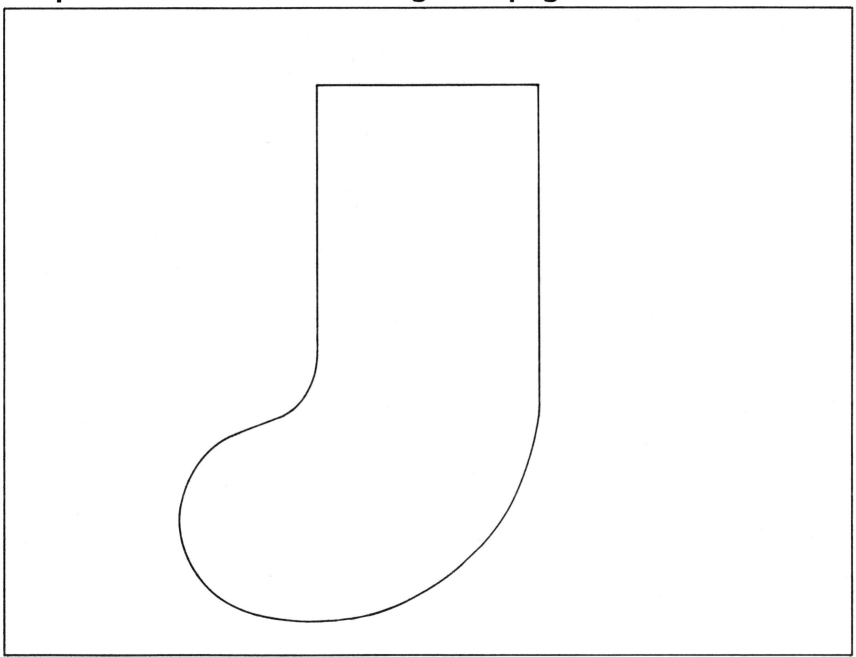

Templates for 'Space dara' baseboard, see page 65

Baseboard for '3 2 1 eggs', see page 68

Baseboard for 'Bear on the stairs', see page 72

Cards for 'Sunflower game', see page 73

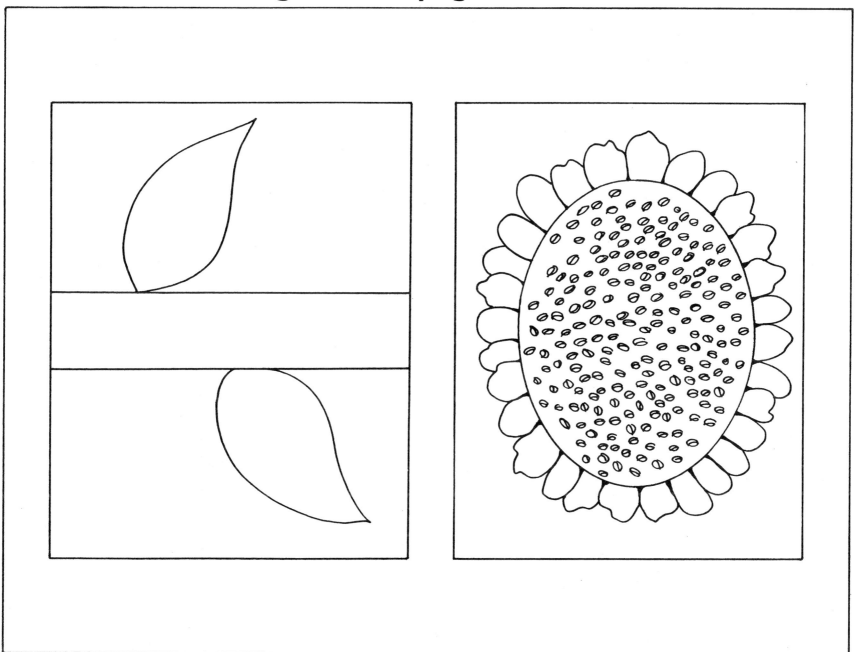

Acknowledgements

All the games in this book were devised and used at Marvels Lane Infant School. Working within the confines of the primary school maths curriculum, it is likely that other teachers will be thinking along the same lines, but any resemblance to games produced elsewhere is purely coincidental.

Our thinking about maths and the use of mathematical games was and continues to be encouraged by Marion Mason, headteacher of Marvels Lane Infant School, and Cathy Murphy, the maths consultant who worked there. Thanks also to the people who ran the maths courses that we attended at the Abbey Wood Maths Centre, and the Lewisham Teachers' Centre for helping us to extend our mathematical thinking.

Other Scholastic books

Bright Ideas
The *Bright Ideas* books provide a wealth of resources for busy primary school teachers. There are now more than 20 titles published, providing clearly explained and illustrated ideas on topics ranging from *Writing* and *Maths Activities* to *Assemblies* and *Christmas Art and Craft*. Each book contains material which can be photocopied for use in the classroom.

Teacher Handbooks
The *Teacher Handbooks* give an overview of the latest research in primary education, and show how it can be put into practice in the classroom. Covering all the core areas of the curriculum, the *Teacher Handbooks* are indispensable to the new teacher as a source of information and useful to the experienced teacher as a quick reference guide.

Management Books
The *Management Books* are designed to help teachers to organise their time, classroom and teaching more efficiently. The books deal with topical issues, such as *Parents and Schools* and organising and planning *Project Teaching*, and are written by authors with lots of practical advice and experiences to share.

Let's Investigate
Let's Investigate is an exciting range of photocopiable activity books giving open-ended investigative tasks. Designed to cover the 6 to 12 year old age range, these books present progressively more difficult concepts and many of the activities can be adapted for use throughout the primary school. Detailed teachers' notes outlining the objectives of each photocopiable sheet and suggesting follow-up activities have been included.